complete
low fat
cooking

complete

low fat

cooking

hamlyn

This edition first published in the U.K. in 1998 by
Hamlyn, a division of Octopus Publishing Group Limited
2–4 Heron Quays, London E14 4JP

ISBN 0 600 60119 6

Printed in Hong Kong

Reprinted 2001

NOTES

All recipes have been analysed by a professional nutritionist. The
analysis refers to each portion. Use in conjunction with the chart
on page 11. The abbreviations are as follows:
kcal=calories; KJ=kilojoules; CHO=carbohydrates

Both metric and imperial measurements have been given in all
recipes. Use one set of measurements, not a mixture of both.

Standard level spoon measurements are used in all recipes.
1 tablespoon = one 15 ml spoon
1 teaspoon = one 5 ml spoon

Eggs should be medium to large unless otherwise stated.
The Department of Health advises that eggs should not be
consumed raw. This book may contain dishes made with raw or
lightly cooked eggs. It is prudent for more vulnerable people such
as pregnant and nursing mothers, invalids, the elderly, babies and
young children to avoid these dishes. Once prepared, these dishes
should be kept refrigerated and used promptly.
Meat and poultry should be cooked thoroughly. To test if poultry
is cooked, pierce the flesh through the thickest part with a skewer
or fork — the juices should run clear, never pink or red. Do not
re-freeze poultry that has been frozen previously and thawed.
Do not re-freeze a cooked dish that has been frozen previously.

Milk should be full fat unless otherwise stated.

Nut and Nut Derivatives
This book includes dishes made with nuts and nut derivatives. It
is advisable for customers with known allergic reactions to nuts
and nut derivatives and those who may be potentially vulnerable
to these allergies, such as pregnant and nursing mothers, invalids,
the elderly, babies and children to avoid dishes made with nuts
and nut oils. It is also prudent to check the labels of pre-prepared
ingredients for the possible inclusion of nut derivatives.

Pepper should be freshly ground black pepper unless otherwise
stated.

Fresh herbs should be used, unless otherwise stated. If
unavailable, use dried herbs as an alternative, but halve the
quantities stated.

Measurements for canned food have been given as a standard
metric equivalent.

Ovens should be pre-heated to the specified temperature
— if using a fan-assisted oven, follow the manufacturer's
instructions for adjusting the time and the temperature.

Vegetarians should look for the 'V' symbol on a cheese to
ensure it is made with vegetarian rennet. There are
vegetarian forms of Parmesan, feta, Cheddar, Cheshire, Red
Leicester, dolcelatte and many goats' cheeses, among others.

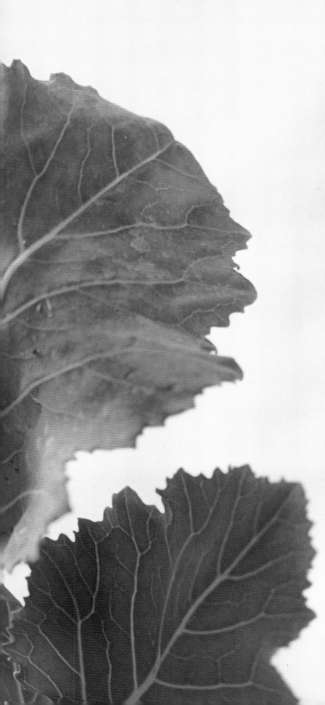

Contents

Introduction

The determination to follow a healthy diet now appears routinely on practically everyone's list of new year resolutions, whether the aim is one of general good health or simply to lose weight. Everyone wants to feel fit and well, and most people would also like to shed a few pounds.

One of the easiest ways of achieving both these admirable aims at one fell swoop is to follow a low-fat diet. This is what this book aims to convince you to do and – still more important – shows you how to do.

Most of us consume more fat today than ever before. The addition of fat gives food a pleasantly rich flavour, as well as a creamy texture that helps it slide satisfyingly down the throat with alarming ease!

But we shouldn't burden ourselves with guilt about our addiction to fat. Apparently we can't help it. Research at the Rockefeller University in the US has shown that the more fat we eat, the more we actually crave, thereby setting up a vicious cycle that it is very hard to escape.

Why reduce fat?

The arguments for reducing the fat in our diet are compelling. Put quite simply, fat is not only fattening, it is also bad for us.

It is believed by some doctors that too high an intake of fat may promote some forms of cancer, particularly colon, prostate and breast cancer. It has also been suggested that eating a lower level of fat may reduce the incidence of atherosclerosis (deposits of excess fat on the artery walls) – thereby decreasing the risk of heart attacks and strokes.

Last but by no means least, particularly for anyone who has trouble maintaining their weight, a low-fat diet will also make it easier to control your weight, especially if you also take regular exercise. Your general health and sense of wellbeing should improve dramatically if you follow a low-fat diet, as well as increasing your general resistance to infection.

Some fat is necessary

Reducing fat does not, however, mean eliminating it completely – even if that were possible. We all need to consume a certain level of fat in a balanced diet. It is essential to our health.

Essential fats, as they are known, are believed to be necessary particularly for certain functions in the body. These include brain function, maintenance of the immune and nervous systems, and regulation of the hormonal balance.

Some forms of fat are much worse than others. Saturated fats, for example, which are solid at room temperature and usually come from animal sources, such as the fat in meat and poultry, butter, lard and cheese, are particularly bad. They tend to encourage the liver to produce more cholesterol, and to make the blood more prone to clotting.

Restrict your intake of fats as much as possible to unsaturated fats – which are liquid at room temperature – such as most vegetable oils (with the exception of coconut

*"The arguments for
reducing the fat in our diet
are compelling."*

oil and palm oil, both of which are saturated fats).
Monounsaturated fats, such as olive oil, are preferable to
polyunsaturated fats, such as safflower and sunflower oils,
as they do not raise blood cholesterol levels.

One particular form of polyunsaturated fat, though,
which is found in fish oils – particularly in oily fish such
as salmon, mackerel, tuna, herring and trout – is
especially good. This is thought to help prevent excessive
blood clotting and are therefore believed to reduce the
risk of heart disease.

To sum up, then, most fats are bad for us and should be
eaten in very small amounts, if at all. A few, however, are
good and some fat is essential for good health. Overall,
though, the best policy is to reduce the general level of all
fat in your diet, and this is what *Complete Low Fat* aims to
show you how to do.

No sacrifice

This book is not about giving up all the delicious things
that we like to eat. Nor is it a faddy diet book. Low-fat

food does not mean making any kind of sacrifice – it can
be just as delicious as its fattier – and, as a result,
unhealthy – counterparts.

Complete Low Fat is, rather, a collection of carefully
planned recipes which allow us to monitor the fats we
consume without compromising on taste. The recipes in
this book have all been carefully devised and nutritionally
analysed so that any cook can find the inspiration to make
delicious meals, which will also contribute to a healthier,
leaner, way of eating.

You will no doubt be surprised – not to say relieved –
to see that there are some old favourites on these pages,
proving that you don't have to give up any of these. You'll
find, for example, classic dishes, such as Traditional Roast
Turkey, Italian Veal Casserole, Tagliatelle Sicilienne and
Strawberry Ice Cream, all of which have been made with a
dramatically reduced fat content, which has in no way
compromised the delicious flavour of the ingredients.

In addition, you will also be pleased to find a great
many interesting and exciting new recipes to add to your
repertoire. Try, for example, Smoked Chicken with Peach
Purée, Chicken with Fresh Mango Sauce, Stuffed Vine
Leaves with Chicken Livers, Haddock and Cider
Casserole, Venison Marinated in Beer, Pumpkin Curry,
Spanish Coleslaw, Couscous with Hot Peppers, Pears with
Fresh Raspberry Sauce and Sliced Figs with Lemon Sauce.
So you thought that low fat eating was boring? Never!
We can guarantee that you will get absolutely no
complaints at all from your taste buds!

"We are not suggesting that you should never eat any of your old favourites ... ever again."

The end of roast beef and Yorkshire pud?

We are not suggesting that you should never eat any of your old favourites, such as roast beef and Yorkshire pudding, ever again. Our traditional idea of wholesome delicious foods is rooted in dishes such as these, and there is absolutely nothing wrong with them – as long as they are consumed IN MODERATION.

But we must bear in mind that the incidence of coronary heart disease has increased dramatically in the past 50 years or so, and that medical research has identified several major causes. One of these is too high a consumption of saturated fats and too high a level of cholesterol in the diet. The foods that many of us eat in the greatest quantities – day in, day out – such as red meat and dairy products, are – sad to say – the biggest culprits of all. These are precisely the foods that we need to eat in smaller quantities.

But that is not as depressing as it sounds. There are, of course, a great many other delicious foods to eat, and this book aims to nudge you persuasively but gently in the right direction.

So what should we eat?

The question of fat in our diets is a complex one. No one single food contains just one type of fat.

It is rather the relative proportion of the different types of fat within any particular food that makes it healthy or unhealthy and that dictates whether or not we should include it in our diet.

What follows is a brief guide to the main food groups available to us – dairy products, meat, fish, fruit and vegetables, and so on – and their value in our diet.

Dairy products

One of the main sources of saturated fats in our diet comes in the form of dairy products, such as milk, butter, cream, cheese and ice cream. Sometimes all you need do is to choose low-fat versions of the usual products that you buy routinely.

Try, for example, to replace whole milk with semi-skimmed or, better still, skimmed milk. Cream substitutes, based on polyunsaturated fats, and low-fat ice-creams can all contribute to lowering our intake of saturated fats. Natural low-fat yogurt and low-fat hard cheese, cottage and curd cheese can also help reduce the level of fat in your diet considerably.

Meat

Watching your fat intake does not mean giving up all meat. But you must be careful about how much of it, and which sort, you eat. Try to limit your portions of meat to about 75 g/3 oz and choose the leanest cuts possible whenever you can.

Remove all traces of visible fat before cooking the meat. It is better to mince very lean cuts of steak, such as sirloin, yourself, or ask your butcher to do it for you, rather than buy prepackaged minced meat, when you have absolutely no control whatsoever over the proportion of fat and lean.

When you roast meat, always place a rack in the bottom of the roasting tin so that the meat does not actually sit in its own juices. Try to roast it for a longer period of time but at a lower temperature – say, 180°C/350°F/Gas Mark 4 – so that the meat is not seared, as this would have the effect of sealing in the fat.

Grilling or griddling are considerably healthier methods of cooking than frying, as they do not need to involve any additional fat. When you grill meat, try

meats. Be careful, though, to choose lean varieties.

Chicken and turkey are a lot leaner, for example, than goose and duck, though the fat in these meats is, at least, rather less saturated than that in red meats. Most of the fat in poultry is found just beneath the skin, so it is advisable always to remove the skin and to trim away all visible fat before cooking.

The best cooking methods are poaching, sautéing, grilling and stir-frying. These are all healthy cooking methods, precisely because they need very little oil. Keep the temperature high and keep the food moving constantly in the wok or pan.

Microwaving is another good way of cooking without adding any extra fat. Indeed, you can actually drain food of extra fat by placing it between two sheets of absorbent kitchen paper while it is cooking.

Fish and shellfish

Fish is often recommended by nutritionists, dieticians and doctors as one of the healthiest foods available. It is an excellent source of protein, while at the same time containing hardly any fat at all. Fish with a particularly low fat content include cod, coley, haddock, whiting and skate. Fish is also generally low in cholesterol. It is therefore an extremely good alternative to meat.

Fatty fish, such as mackerel, herring, sardines, tuna, salmon and trout, are all excellent sources of polyunsaturated oils, which are believed to have a particularly protective effect on the circulation by making the blood platelets less sticky and consequently less liable to clot. This explains why the Inuit, who eat particularly large quantities of fish on a regular basis, have such a low incidence of heart disease.

According to many nutritionists and doctors, it is a good idea to eat fish at least two or three times a week, and to eat fatty fish at least once a week. If you like to eat canned fish, such as sardines, salmon or tuna, read the labels carefully when you buy them and choose those that have been preserved in brine or in a named, healthy oil, such as soya, sunflower or olive, rather than in an unnamed 'vegetable' oil which is probably of inferior quality.

Steaming, poaching and microwaving are all good methods of cooking fresh fish. Cooking whole fish in

adding extra flavour by marinating it first in herbs, wine, garlic, and tomato or lemon juice. Barbecuing is another healthy method of cooking, which is practically the same as grilling, and is a good way to cook in summer when you can move your cooking paraphernalia outside.

If you casserole or stew meat, it is always a good idea, if at all possible, to cook it on the day before you actually want to eat it. Chill the stew after cooking it, then skim off any solidified fat before you complete the cooking time or reheat it just before eating.

Sausages and processed meats often contain a high proportion of hidden fats – you can't actually see them but they're there! – which have been added as part of the preparation. To avoid these as much as possible, always read the labels carefully before buying and try to select those that have no more than 10% fat by weight.

Poultry and game

Poultry, or white meat, and game, such as rabbit, venison, pigeon, partridge and pheasant, are nearly always a lot lower in fat than red meat and contain a lot more polyunsaturated fat and less saturated fat than other parcels of greaseproof paper or kitchen foil with seasonings, herbs and flavourings is a highly recommended way of preparing it as it seals in all the flavour without the need to add any extra fat during the cooking process.

A lot of shellfish, such as prawns, lobster and crab, are very low in fat, although weight for weight some types of shellfish, such as prawns, actually contain a higher level of cholesterol than meat and poultry. However, even these can be eaten occasionally without causing any risk to a person's health.

Fruits, vegetables, grains and legumes

These foods contain absolutely no cholesterol and tend to be low in fat and high in fibre and vitamins. It is true that olives and avocados are exceptions and are both high in fat but, as the fat is largely unsaturated, their intake needs to be limited only for their high calorie count.

Be careful to check the labels of processed foods made from vegetables, grains or legumes for fats that have been added during processing. Breads and pastas made with egg yolks should be avoided because the egg also increases their fat content. You should also check that processed vegetables have not had sodium, or salt, added during their preparation. Ideally, as a general rule, fresh produce is always better than processed foods.

Vegetables and salads come in an enormous variety and can be prepared in a great many different ways. Steamed vegetables contain no fat at all and a fresh green salad can be heaped on the plate in virtually unlimited quantities with no oil added to the dressing for a healthy, slimming meal.

Nuts and seeds

A lot of people like to include nuts and seeds in their diet as snacks, but they should be careful. These foods tend to be very high in their fat content and can therefore be correspondingly – and alarmingly – high in calories.

The news is not all bad, though, as nuts and seeds do not contain any cholesterol and their fats are usually unsaturated. They also tend to be high in vitamins and minerals.

So eat them by all means, but – as always – it is advisable to exercise a little moderation, especially if you are keen not to put on any extra weight.

Cakes, pastries, crackers and crisp breads

Cakes and pastries tend to be high in calories and fat and not of any great nutritional value. If you must eat cakes, it is always better to make your own rather than to eat bought ones. When you bake at home, you should always use a healthy, polyunsaturated oil rather than butter,

> *"... it is a good idea to get into the habit of studying food labels carefully."*

The recommended proportions of various nutrients are shown in this table below.

RECOMMENDED NUTRIENT INTAKE

Total fat 35% of total energy (kcal)
(E.g. in a 2,000 calorie diet, not more than 700 calories should come from fat. This equals 80 g fat per day, or 40 g fat for every 1,000 calories.)
Saturated fatty acids Less than 10% of total energy (kcal)
Polyunsaturated fatty acids Up to 10% of total energy (kcal)
Monounsaturated fatty acids 10–15% of total energy (kcal)
Carbohydrate 50% of total calories
Protein 10–20% of total calories
Total calories Keep an eye on these in order to achieve and maintain your desirable weight

---

and substitute egg whites for some of the yolks.

Read the labels on any packets of manufactured crackers and crisp breads before you buy them, as they are often coated in vegetable oil before crisping and may actually be much higher in fat than you think. Bought biscuits and cakes are often rich in hidden fats, which are usually saturated, so again, read the labels carefully and make your choice accordingly.

Choosing your foods

Nowadays, many of the foods that you will find on sale in the supermarkets are labelled with their carbohydrate, fat, protein and calorie content. This is a very useful guide and it is therefore a good idea to get into the habit of studying food labels carefully. If you do this, it can then become automatic to calculate a recommended daily intake of all the main nutrient groups.

Cooking methods

Whenever possible, it is better to grill or bake than to fry foods, and to use no additional fat. If you do fry, make sure that you use an unsaturated oil rather than butter or lard, and cook in a non-stick pan so that you need only the tiniest amount of oil in order to prevent the food from sticking.

Steaming and microwaving are also excellent methods of cooking. They are not only healthy methods, but they also retain a good deal of the food's flavour, texture and colour, so that it is not only good for you but it also looks and tastes good, too. Whatever you do, be careful not to add any extra fat, which would defeat the purpose.

Cook's tools

> *"Give me neither poverty nor riches;*
> *feed me with food convenient to me."*
>
> *Proverbs: Ecclesiastes*

Mixing bowl

A mixing bowl should be wide enough to allow mixtures to be beaten or folded. The bowl should be rested on a grip stand or a cloth to prevent it slipping.

Sieve

A sieve has a rigid frame and a mesh dome in variations from fine to coarse. It can be used for separating solids from liquids, solids from solids, and also for refining ingredients. The mesh should be stainless steel to prevent rust.

Vegetable masher

A masher is used to mash cooked starchy vegetables, such as potatoes, swedes and carrots.

Whisk

A whisk is an essential beating tool used to blend ingredients and incorporate air into batter or other mixtures. Whisks come in different shapes and sizes – small ones are used for sauces, though the larger balloon whisk is the most popular and commonly used. They are very handy for rescuing a lumpy sauce.

Pasta server

A pasta server is a large stainless steel spoon with a long handle, used for transferring pasta or noodles from the pan to the serving dish. It has characteristic teeth which enable you to pick up spaghetti and tagliatelle easily and a hole which lets the liquid drain away.

Lemon squeezers

Lemon squeezers are used for extracting the juice from a lemon. One type is designed to work on half a lemon, while the other is meant to be used on lemon wedges and is less messy than doing it by hand. Lemon squeezers are made of stainless steel or plastic.

Knives

A good cook is not properly equipped without a set of sharp knives. They should be well maintained, cleaned and dried thoroughly, and sharpened regularly.

Garlic crusher

A garlic crusher is used to crush garlic finely by forcing the flesh through small holes. This releases the oils and the full flavour of the garlic. This useful tool saves the pungent aroma of garlic lingering on your skin, as you do not have to handle the juices from the garlic.

Measuring jugs

A measuring jug is a standardized measure of liquid. It has a handle and a good pouring lip. Normally it is marked in both metric and imperial measures, fractions of pints and fluid ounces, as well as millilitres and litres. Jugs are available in glass, stainless steel and plastic. Always check before buying a measuring jug that it is dishwasher proof.

Measuring cups

These are quick and easy to use, though measuring dry goods by volume is not as accurate as measuring by weight.

Soups and Starters

Celeriac and Apple Soup

25 g/1 oz butter or margarine
1 celeriac, about 500 g/1 lb, peeled and chopped
3 dessert apples, peeled, cored and chopped
1.2 litres/2 pints Chicken or Vegetable Stock (see page 244)
pinch of cayenne pepper, or more to taste
salt and ground white pepper

Garnish
2–3 tablespoons finely diced dessert apple
paprika

melt the butter or margarine in a large saucepan and cook the celeriac and apples over a moderate heat for 5 minutes or until the vegetables have begun to soften.

add the stock and cayenne pepper and bring to the boil. Lower the heat and simmer, covered, for 25–30 minutes, or until the celeriac and apples are very soft.

purée the mixture in batches in a blender or food processor, until it is very smooth, transferring each successive batch to a clean saucepan. Reheat gently. Season to taste with salt and pepper. Serve hot in heated soup bowls or plates. Garnish each portion with the finely diced apple and a dusting of paprika.

Serves 6
Preparation time: *10–15 minutes*
Cooking time: *about 35 minutes*

kcal 58 • KJ 243 • protein 1 g • fat 4 g • CHO 6 g

clipboard: Cayenne, or red pepper, is made from the dried and ground flesh and seeds of the bird's eye chilli. It is similar to chilli powder but not usually as hot. Paprika is made from mild varieties of capsicum, or sweet pepper, which have had their seeds removed before being dried and ground. It should be bought in small amounts and replaced often as it loses both flavour and colour remarkably quickly.

Rice Noodle Soup

750 ml / 1 ¼ pints Vegetable Stock (see page 244)
3 spring onions, cut into 2.5 cm / 1 inch lengths
2 baby corns, sliced obliquely
1 tomato, quartered
1 onion, cut into 8 pieces
6 lime leaves, shredded
1 celery stick, chopped
½ x 250 g / 8 oz block ready-steamed tofu, diced
1 tablespoon soy sauce
1 teaspoon ground black pepper
1–2 teaspoons crushed dried chillies
175 g / 6 oz dried wide rice noodles, soaked and drained

Garnish
fresh coriander leaves, cut into strips
lime quarters

heat the stock in a saucepan and add all of the ingredients except for the noodles.

bring to the boil for 30 seconds, then lower the heat to a simmer and cook for 5 minutes.

add the noodles and simmer for another 2 minutes.

pour into a serving bowl, garnished with coriander sprigs, and serve with lime quarters.

Serves 4
Preparation time: *10 minutes, plus 15–20 minutes soaking time*
Cooking time: *8 minutes*

kcal 227 • KJ 951 • protein 9 g • fat 3 g • CHO 40 g

clipboard: Lime leaves give food an intense lemon aroma. They can be bought dried, in which case half the quantity stated should be used, or fresh, which will keep for several weeks in the refrigerator. They are frequently used in Indonesian, Thai and other southeast Asian dishes. Rice noodles are sold in packets at supermarkets and Chinese food stores. They cook quickly and are a particularly tasty and filling addition to a soup of this sort.

Green Garden Soup

This soup is a hearty broth made with a selection of fresh vegetables — celery, leeks, watercress, lettuce, spring onions and fennel. It's as good for you as it is delicious to eat.

4 celery sticks, chopped
2 leeks, cleaned and chopped
I bunch watercress, washed and chopped
I heart of a round lettuce, shredded
4 spring onions, chopped
I tablespoon chopped fresh tarragon
I garlic clove, peeled and crushed
I small head fennel, shredded
600 ml/I pint Chicken Stock (see page 244)
300 ml/½ pint skimmed milk
50 g/2 oz fine green fettucine, broken into short lengths
salt and freshly ground black pepper

put the celery, leeks, watercress, lettuce, spring onions, tarragon, garlic, and fennel into a large pan; add the stock, skimmed milk and salt and pepper to taste.

simmer the soup for 20–25 minutes until all the vegetables are tender.

blend the soup in a liquidiser until smooth.

return the soup to a clean pan and bring to the boil. Add the broken fettucine and simmer for about 4 minutes, until the pasta is just tender. Serve the soup piping hot.

Serves 4
Preparation time: *15 minutes*
Cooking time: *about 30 minutes*

kcal 108 •KJ 460 • protein 8 g • fat 1 g • CHO 18 g

Chilled Pea Soup

A chilled soup is always a refreshingly welcome dish to serve in the summer months, when the weather is hot. This lemony pea soup, garnished with chopped fresh mint, is just the ticket.

375 g/12 oz fresh shelled peas or frozen petit pois
250 g/8 oz potatoes, chopped
1 onion, chopped
1 large sprig of mint
finely grated rind of ½ lemon
2 tablespoons lemon juice
900 ml/1½ pints Chicken Stock (see page 244)
salt and pepper
1 tablespoon chopped fresh mint, to garnish

place the peas in a large saucepan with the potatoes, onion, mint sprig, lemon rind and juice and stock and season with salt and pepper. Bring to the boil, lower heat, cover and simmer for 15–20 minutes or until the peas are tender.

purée in a blender or press through a sieve. Set aside to cool.

adjust the seasoning to taste and chill in the refrigerator for 2–3 hours. Serve chilled, sprinkled with the mint.

Serves 4
Preparation time: *20 minutes, plus chilling*
Cooking time: *15–20 minutes*

kcal 106 • KJ 447 • protein 6 g • fat 1 g • CHO 18 g

clipboard: Mint is one of the most popular herbs for use in the kitchen. It is a member of the same family as sage, thyme, marjoram, oregano, rosemary, basil, savory and lemon balm. Its flavour goes particularly well with peas and potatoes, both of which are used in this recipe.

Salad leaves

Chinese leaves

Rocket

Little Gem

Curly leaf

Chinese leaves

Chinese leaves originated in southeast Asia several hundred years ago. They are pale green, tightly packed leaves which form a long, thin, tapering cabbage. They have a clean delicate flavour and can be used as a steamed vegetable or in salads and stir-fries.

Rocket

Originally from Europe, rocket was a popular kitchen herb in Elizabethan and Stuart times and has enjoyed a great revival in popularity in the last few years. It has a slightly peppery flavour and is good eaten raw in salads as well as being added to pasta dishes.

Little Gem

Little Gem is a small loose-leaf lettuce, which has crisp, slightly crinkled little leaves in a pale green colour. It is of more interest for its crispness than its flavour, which is rather bland. It is a popular salad green, and also makes a good garnish. It has no heart.

Curly leaf

Curly leaf lettuce is a crisp, fresh, pale green lettuce with loose leaves, which is particularly good used either in a green salad or as a garnish. It has good keeping qualities and will last well for several days in the salad drawer of the refrigerator.

Radicchio

Lamb's lettuce

Chicory

Frisée

Radicchio

These crisp, dark pinkish red leaves with crisp white ribs look absolutely wonderful in a salad, especially when combined with other salad 'greens'. They have a distinctive flavour and make an attractive garnish. They can also be grilled or fried.

Lamb's lettuce

Also known as corn salad or mâche, lamb's lettuce has a pleasantly mild, slightly nutty flavour and is excellent in salads, either on its own or in combination with other salad greens. Its delicate little leaves look good when used as a garnish, too.

Chicory

Also known as Belgian endive, this is a very compact cone-shaped salad vegetable with long, slightly crisp, yellow-tipped leaves. It can be cooked or used in salads, too. The roots are also roasted, ground and used as a substitute for coffee.

Frisée

Also known as curly endive, frisée has attractive lacy leaves, which are various shades of green, yellow and even white. It is a member of the chicory family and has a slightly bitter taste, which some people do not find agreeable. It makes an attractive garnish, too.

Italian Leek and Pumpkin Soup

The hollowed-out shell of the pumpkin can be used to make an impressive tureen in which to serve this soup.

1 Spanish onion, chopped
50 g/2 oz leek, chopped
600 ml/1 pint hot Chicken Stock (see page 244)
500 g/1 lb pumpkin flesh
250 g/8 oz potatoes
600 ml/1 pint skimmed milk
125 g/4 oz long-grain rice, cooked
150 ml/¼ pint low-fat natural yogurt
salt and freshly ground black pepper
chopped parsley, to garnish

soften the onion and leek in 2 tablespoons of the stock. Dice the pumpkin flesh and potatoes and add, with the seasoning, the milk and the remaining stock, to the onions. Bring to the boil, cover and simmer for 45 minutes, stirring frequently.

blend the soup in a liquidizer or press through a sieve. Return to the pan and add the cooked rice and most of the yogurt. Reheat gently. Serve, topped with the remaining yogurt and sprinkled with parsley.

Serves 8
Preparation time: *30 minutes*
Cooking time: *45 minutes*

kcal 90 •KJ 380 • protein 5 g • fat 1 g • CHO 16 g

clipboard: Pumpkin has a golden, nutty-flavoured flesh and a centre filled with edible seeds. There are numerous varieties, which can be served steamed, boiled, baked and stuffed.

French Onion Soup

French onion soup is a classic recipe, which is traditionally served with its characteristic slices of cheesy toast on top.

3 large Spanish onions, finely chopped
1.2 litres/2 pints beef stock, made with 2 stock cubes
1 teaspoon sugar
6 slices French bread
125 g/4 oz reduced-fat Edam cheese, grated
1 tablespoon brandy
salt and freshly ground black pepper
chopped parsley, to garnish (optional)

cook the onions in some of the stock in a heavy-bottomed covered pan for at least 30 minutes, turning frequently. They should not brown but should be quite soft. Add the rest of the stock, the sugar, salt and pepper, and boil for a further 30 minutes.

meanwhile, toast the bread slices in the oven, heap the grated cheese on top and brown under the grill. Now stir the brandy into the soup and serve, with a cheesy bread slice in each bowl. Sprinkle with chopped parsley, if liked.

Serves 6
Preparation time: *20 minutes*
Cooking time: *1 hour*

kcal 125 •KJ 526 • protein 8 g • fat 3 g • CHO 16 g

Fresh Tomato Soup

This recipe for tomato soup is not only simple, it is also delicious. The subtle orange flavour really does make all the difference to this popular soup.

1 kg/2 lb ripe tomatoes, roughly chopped
1 small onion, chopped
1 tablespoon vegetable oil
1 sugar cube
1 orange
1.8 litres/3 pints Chicken or Vegetable Stock
(see page 244)
2 cloves
bouquet garni
fresh thyme leaves, to garnish

soften the tomatoes and onion in the oil for about 8 minutes. Rub the sugar cube over the orange peel, to absorb the zest, and add with the remaining ingredients to the tomato mixture. Bring to the boil, cover and simmer gently for 25 minutes. Remove the cloves and bouquet garni.

blend the soup in a liquidizer, then push with a wooden spoon through a fine sieve. Reheat and serve, garnished with thyme leaves.

Serves 8
Preparation time: *20 minutes*
Cooking time: *35 minutes*

kcal 50 • KJ 210 • protein 2 g
• fat 2 g • CHO 7 g

clipboard: A bouquet garni usually consists of a bay leaf, a sprig of thyme and 3 stalks of parsley. It is often enclosed in a piece of celery stick or a piece of leek, tied with string, or it can be wrapped in a small square of muslin, tied with thin string.

Young Vegetables

with Garlic Sauce

Use an adventurous selection of seasonal vegetables: steamed young courgettes, carrots, baby sweetcorn, white cabbage, cauliflower and mushrooms. Cold new potatoes in their skins taste especially good with the garlic sauce. Lightly steam the vegetables or leave them raw, according to taste.

about 1.25 kg/2½ lb raw and/or cooked vegetables

Sauce
3–4 large garlic cloves, peeled and roughly chopped
1 teaspoon salt
2–3 tablespoons lemon juice
4 tablespoons tahini (sesame seed paste)
freshly ground black pepper
1 teaspoon olive oil
2 teaspoons finely chopped fresh parsley or coriander

prepare the vegetables, trimming and steaming as necessary.

make the sauce. Using a pestle and mortar, reduce the garlic to a pulp with the salt, then add the lemon juice.

slowly incorporate the mixture into the tahini, adding enough water to make a consistency similar to that of thick cream.

taste and adjust the seasoning with salt, pepper or lemon juice. Finally stir in the oil and parsley or coriander. Transfer to a small bowl.

arrange the vegetables on a platter. Serve with the garlic sauce on the side for easy dipping.

Serves 8
Preparation time: *about 30 minutes*
Cooking time: *according to vegetables*

kcal 82 • KJ 340 • protein 4 g • fat 5 g • CHO 6 g

Smoked Chicken
with Peach Purée

3 ripe peaches
3 tablespoons dry vermouth
1 teaspoon French mustard
1 teaspoon chopped fresh tarragon
12 thin slices smoked chicken, about 175–250 g/
6–8 oz in total
salt and freshly ground black pepper

Garnish
thin slices of fresh peach
small sprigs of fresh tarragon

nick the stalk end of each peach. Plunge into a bowl of boiling water for 45 seconds, then slide off the skins. Remove the stones and chop the flesh.

blend the peach flesh in a liquidizer with the vermouth, mustard, chopped tarragon, and a little salt and pepper.

cover the sauce and chill for 1 hour. (Do not chill any longer in order to avoid discoloration.)

spoon a little of the sauce on to each plate, and lay 3 slices of chicken in a fan shape close by.

garnish with thin slices of peach and with sprigs of fresh tarragon.

Serves 4
Preparation time: *25 minutes, plus chilling*

kcal 120 • KJ 570 • protein 15 g • fat 3 g • CHO 7 g

clipboard: Tarragon has a special affinity with chicken. French tarragon has a strong, clear flavour and is preferable to Russian tarragon, which has virtually no taste at all. Tarragon is easy to grow from cuttings, but it should be lifted every year and planted in a fresh spot, as it uses up all the trace elements in the soil and the flavour will therefore deteriorate.

Stuffed Vine Leaves

These vine leaves are stuffed with a delicious combination of chicken livers, rice and pine kernels. Vine leaves are available in cans.

2 teaspoons vegetable oil

1 medium onion, peeled and chopped

1 clove garlic, crushed

75 g/3 oz chicken livers

125 g/4 oz cooked rice

25 g/1 oz pine kernels

36 canned vine leaves

about 300 ml/½ pint Chicken Stock (see page 244)

salt and freshly ground black pepper

heat the oil in a frying pan and fry the onion and garlic until soft and transparent. Add the chicken livers and fry for a further 3 minutes, stirring constantly, until lightly browned on all sides. Remove the livers from the pan and chop finely. Place the rice in a bowl and add the livers, onion, garlic and pan juices, the pine kernels and salt and pepper to taste. Mix well.

lay the vine leaves on a work surface with the underside of the leaves uppermost. Put a teaspoon of the rice mixture on each leaf and roll them up, tucking the sides in, to make a neat parcel. Place the leaves close together in a casserole, making two or more layers.

pour in enough stock to come halfway up the sides of the casserole and just cover the vine leaves. Cover and place in a preheated moderate oven at 180°C/350°F/Gas Mark 4 for 30–40 minutes until cooked through. Serve at once, or leave until cold.

Serves 6–8
Preparation time: *30 minutes*
Cooking time: *30–40 minutes*
Oven temperature: 180°C/350°F/Gas
  Mark 4

*kcal 98 •KJ 411 • protein 7 g
• fat 5 g • CHO 7 g*

Bean and Mushroom Salad

1 kg/2 lb frozen whole French beans
500 g/1 lb button mushrooms
juice of ½ lemon
½ small onion, grated
a little ground coriander
3 tablespoons chopped parsley
300 ml/½ pint Low-Calorie French Dressing (see page 246)
salt

cook the beans in boiling salted water until just tender, then cool under running water. Drain thoroughly.

wipe the mushrooms with a clean damp cloth and slice finely. Sprinkle with lemon juice. Add the onion, ground coriander and parsley to the French dressing, then pour over the mushrooms. Leave to marinate for 1 or 2 hours, turning gently from time to time.

toss the mushroom mixture carefully with the French beans and serve in a large serving dish or on individual plates.

Serves 8
Preparation time: *10 minutes, plus 1 or 2 hours marinating*
Cooking time: *8–15 minutes*

kcal 60 • KJ 250 • protein 4 g • fat 1 g • CHO 9 g

clipboard: French beans and mushrooms are a particularly successful combination. Fresh beans may be used instead of frozen ones, if you prefer.

Salads

Glass Noodle Salad

200 g/7 oz dried glass noodles, soaked and drained
1 tomato, halved and sliced
20 g/¾ oz celery stick, chopped
20 g/¾ oz spring onion, chopped
1 onion, halved and sliced
50 g/2 oz green pepper, cored, deseeded and chopped
juice of 2 limes
5 small green chillies, finely chopped
2 teaspoons sugar
25 g/1 oz crushed roasted peanuts
1 teaspoon crushed dried chillies
½ teaspoon salt
2½ teaspoons *nam pla* or fish sauce
fresh coriander sprigs, to garnish

cook the noodles in boiling water for 3–4 minutes, then drain and rinse them under cold water to prevent further cooking.

cut the noodles into 12 cm/5 inch lengths. Return them to the pan and add all the remaining ingredients. Mix thoroughly for 2 minutes.

serve at room temperature, garnished with fresh coriander sprigs.

Serves 4
Preparation time: *15 minutes, plus soaking*
Cooking time: *3–4 minutes*

kcal 240 • KJ 1016 • protein 9 g • fat 4 g • CHO 44 g

clipboard: To make crushed roasted peanuts, dry-fry the nuts in a frying pan until they turn a golden colour, then allow to cool. Place them in a plastic bag and break into small pieces using a rolling pin. *Nam pla* is a salty, spiced, fermented fish mixture, and is available from Oriental food stores and some supermarkets.

Mushroom, Courgette and Tomato Salad

6 large mushrooms, sliced
4 courgettes, thinly sliced
4 tomatoes, peeled and quartered
I teaspoon chopped fresh basil
I bunch mustard and cress, trimmed and divided into sprigs
3 tablespoons Low-Calorie French Dressing (see page 246), to serve

combine the mushrooms, courgettes and tomatoes in a salad bowl and sprinkle with the basil.

arrange the sprigs of mustard and cress round the edge of the salad. Serve with Low-Calorie French Dressing.

Serves 4
Preparation time: *15 minutes*

kcal 50 • KJ 213 • protein 3 g • fat 1 g • CHO 8 g

clipboard: A combination of contrasting colours gives a salad visual appeal and makes the mouth water in anticipation. Mushrooms, courgettes and tomatoes not only look good together, they also complement each other in taste.

Provençal Pasta Salad

175 g/6 oz rigatoni or penne
4 tablespoons low-fat mayonnaise
juice of ½ lemon
6 tomatoes, skinned, deseeded and chopped
125 g/4 oz French beans, cooked
12 black olives, pitted
1 x 200 g/7 oz can tuna in brine, drained and flaked
salt and pepper
1 x 50 g/2 oz can anchovy fillets, drained and washed, to garnish
1 small head lettuce, shredded, to serve

bring a large saucepan of salted water to the boil. Add the pasta, stir and cook for 10–12 minutes until *al dente*. Drain the pasta well and mix with a little of the dressing.

allow the pasta to cool, turn into a bowl and mix with the lemon juice, tomatoes, beans, olives and flaked tuna and season with salt and pepper.

toss the salad lightly in the remaining dressing and serve on a bed of shredded lettuce and garnished with anchovies.

Serves 6
Preparation time: *10–12 minutes, plus cooling*
Cooking time: *about 12 minutes*

Kcal 198 • KJ 839 • protein 14 g • fat 5 g • CHO 26 g

Apple and Walnut Salad

Salads made with fruit and nuts make a refreshing change from the usual salad ingredients and add an interesting variation in texture as well as flavour.

1 iceberg lettuce, sliced
2 bunches watercress, trimmed and chopped
1 apple, peeled, cubed and tossed in lemon juice
25 g/1 oz walnuts, chopped
1 tablespoon walnut oil
2 tablespoons wine vinegar
salt and freshly ground black pepper

mix the lettuce with the watercress and apple.

sprinkle the walnuts over and drizzle on the walnut oil and vinegar. Season with salt and pepper. Toss the salad well just before serving.

Serves 6
Preparation time: *15–20 minutes*

kcal 65 • KJ 268 • protein 2 g • fat 5 g • CHO 3 g

clipboard: The partnership of apples with walnuts was made in heaven, but other fruit and nut combinations can work equally well. In the summer months, try peach and hazelnuts with hazelnut oil, for example, or apricots and almonds.

Tricolour Salad

Bright colours and contrasting textures make this salad a refreshing antidote to the end of winter. For the best flavour, serve at room temperature, not chilled.

125 g/4 oz leeks, trimmed and sliced into rings
125 g/4 oz red pepper, cored, deseeded and diced
2 medium oranges, about 250 g/8 oz flesh, peeled and cut into quartered slices
1 tablespoon chopped fresh dill
1 tablespoon chopped fresh parsley
150 ml/¼ pint natural low-fat yogurt
1 teaspoon clear honey
freshly ground black pepper
sprig of fresh dill, to garnish

combine the prepared leeks, red pepper and oranges in a serving dish.

blend together the dill, parsley, yogurt, honey and pepper and pour over the salad. Garnish with the sprig of dill.

Serves 4
Preparation time: *10 minutes*

kcal 63 • KJ 268 • protein 3 g • fat 1 g • CHO 12 g

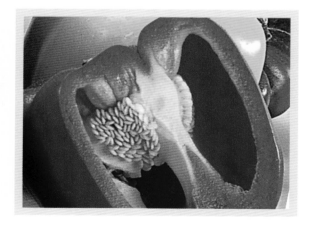

clipboard: Dill is a rather tall herb which grows up to 60 cm/2 feet high. It has hollow stems, thin thread-like leaves and umbels of yellow flowers. It looks very similar to fennel. It goes particularly well with fish and in soups, cream sauces, salads, vegetable dishes and pickles.

Spanish Coleslaw

This is coleslaw with a difference, with the addition of green and red peppers and grapes. It's a colourful salad, which looks as interesting as it tastes.

250 g/8 oz white cabbage, finely shredded
I small onion, finely chopped
½ green pepper, cored, deseeded and chopped
½ red pepper, cored, deseeded and chopped
I large carrot, grated
50 g/2 oz grapes, halved and seeded
6 tablespoons natural low-fat yogurt
I tablespoon Low-calorie French Dressing
(see page 246)
salt and pepper
chopped parsley, to garnish

place the cabbage in a bowl and add the onion, green and red peppers, carrot and grapes.

mix together the yogurt and dressing. Season with salt and pepper to taste. Add to the vegetables and toss thoroughly. Transfer to a serving bowl and garnish with chopped parsley.

Serves 4
Preparation time: *20 minutes*

kcal 65 • KJ 273 • protein 4 g • fat 1 g • CHO 12 g

Spinach, Mushroom and Hazelnut Salad

The combination of flavours and textures in this salad makes for a very interesting dish, which would make a superb starter.

2 teaspoons olive oil
2 tablespoons white wine vinegar
1 garlic clove, peeled and chopped
2 tablespoons roughly chopped parsley
3 tablespoons plain yogurt
175 g/6 oz young fresh spinach leaves, washed and shaken
125 g/4 oz button mushrooms, thinly sliced
25 g/1 oz hazelnuts, coarsely chopped
salt and freshly ground black pepper

to make the dressing, blend together the olive oil, wine vinegar, garlic, parsley, yogurt, and salt and pepper to taste in a liquidiser until smooth.

tear the spinach leaves into pieces and divide these among 6 individual salad plates.

scatter the mushrooms and hazelnuts over the spinach. Spoon the prepared dressing over each serving, and toss lightly.

Serves 6
Preparation time: *15 minutes*

kcal 57 • KJ 238 • protein 3 g • fat 4 g • CHO 3 g

Herbs and spices

Dill

Chervil

Rosemary

Basil

Thyme

Marjoram

Dill

Dill is an annual herb from Europe and grows to about 60 cm/2 feet. It has hollow stems, feathery thread-like leaves, umbels of yellow flowers, and seeds that look rather like caraway seeds. The plant is almost indistinguishable in appearance from fennel. The seeds are believed to aid the digestion. It is particularly good with fish and is also used in many soups, sauces and salads.

Basil

Basil is a delicious summer herb with an intense aroma and a distinctive flavour. It is the main ingredient in pesto sauce, which is a popular Italian basil sauce often served with pasta. Basil also has a great affinity with tomatoes. It does not respond very well to heat and is therefore best added to dishes at the end of cooking, used as a garnish, or added to cold dishes such as salads.

Chervil

Chervil originated in the Middle East and southern Russia and was probably introduced into Europe by the Romans. It is a biennial plant growing to about 40 cm/16 inches, with fern-like leaves and small white flowers with little black seed pods. It is especially good in soups, with chicken, fish, salads and eggs. It is best added once the cooking is over as it does not respond well to heat.

Thyme

Thyme is a bushy shrub with grey-green leaves and pink, mauve, red or white flowers. It has a fragrant aroma and a clove-like flavour. It can be bought fresh or dried, combines well with other herbs and can withstand long cooking.

Rosemary

Rosemary is a perennial herb with long spiky green leaves and pale blue flowers. It can be bought fresh or dried, and is also easy to cultivate at home. When it is fresh, it is strongly flavoured and aromatic. It is often used to flavour vinegars and oils.

Marjoram

Sweet marjoram, which is the more commonly used variety, has a warm, delicate flavour and is good with tomatoes and in pasta, chicken and vegetable dishes. It is best added when the cooking is finished.

Nutmeg

Root ginger

Lemon grass

Saffron

Red chillies

Kaffir lime leaves

Saffron
Made from the dried stigmas of the crocus plant, saffron is the most expensive of all spices. It is available either as whole threads or ground into a powder. The threads are generally considered to be better.

Nutmeg
The nutmeg tree originally grew in the Molucca Islands, where it formed a valuable part of the spice trade. The seed of the tree grows within a lacy cage of mace and is dried in the sun after harvesting. It is sold both whole and ground. It is best bought whole as the powdered variety soon loses its fragrance. It is good in milk-based puddings and sauces, in vegetable dishes and in fruit cakes.

Red chillies
Dried red chillies are available whole or crushed. They are extremely fiery and must therefore be used with caution. Removing the seeds tones down some of their heat. Be careful to wash your hands after handling chillies and not to touch your eyes, as it can sting.

Root ginger
A thick knobbly root with pale brown skin and moist golden-coloured flesh, this has a slightly hot, pungent flavour, which is particularly well suited to Indian and Asian cooking. Dried and ground, it can also be used to add a little spice to cakes and desserts.

Lemon grass
In its fresh state, lemon grass is considered to be a herb, but when it is dried, whether whole or powdered, it is considered to be a spice. Its flavour is reminiscent of lemon rind, and it is an important ingredient in southeast Asian cuisine. The whole dried stem should be soaked before being used in cooking, whereas the powdered kind does not require soaking and is therefore easier to use.

Kaffir lime leaves
Strongly citrus flavoured, these are available fresh or dried in Oriental food stores and large supermarkets. They are commonly used in Indonesian, Thai and other southeast Asian cookery. Lime or lemon rind may be used as an acceptable substitute if lime leaves are not available.

Brown Rice and Mixed Herb Salad

1 small onion, peeled and finely chopped
1 garlic clove, peeled and finely chopped
½ teaspoon garam masala
150 g/5 oz long-grain brown rice
pinch of powdered saffron
400 ml/14 fl oz Chicken Stock (see page 244)
½ tablespoon desiccated coconut
2 teaspoons olive oil
2 tablespoons tarragon vinegar
1 tablespoon chopped coriander
2 tablespoons chopped parsley
10 cashew nuts, lightly toasted
salt and freshly ground black pepper

dry-fry the onion gently for 3 minutes; add the garlic, garam masala and rice, and fry gently for a further 2 minutes, stirring continuously.

stir in the saffron, chicken stock, desiccated coconut, and salt and pepper to taste. Bring to the boil and simmer gently for about 25 minutes, until the rice is just tender.

mix the olive oil with the tarragon vinegar, the coriander and parsley, and season to taste. Stir evenly through the warm rice, together with the cashew nuts.

allow to cool before serving.

Serves 4
Preparation time: *10 minutes, plus chilling*
Cooking time: *30–35 minutes*

kcal 184 • KJ 777 • protein 4 g • fat 5 g • CHO 33 g

clipboard: The quality of brown rice varies enormously and some types absorb more liquid while cooking than others, so check from time to time to see that the rice is not becoming too dry and, if necessary, add some extra chicken stock. Garam masala is a traditional Indian spice mixture, which is available ready-prepared. It usually includes cardamom, cloves, cinnamon, black pepper, and perhaps nutmeg.

Vegetables

Artichokes Provençal

For such an ugly-looking vegetable, Jerusalem artichokes have a surprisingly delicate flavour. They are on sale in winter and spring and are very nutritious, being rich in phosphorus and potassium.

I kg/2 lb Jerusalem artichokes, scraped
2 large cloves garlic, crushed
500 g/I lb tomatoes, peeled, seeded and chopped
2 tablespoons tomato purée
juice of ½ lemon
I tablespoon chopped fresh basil
or ½ teaspoon dried
I teaspoon sugar
2 tablespoons chopped parsley
salt and freshly ground black pepper

slice the artichokes thickly and steam or poach them for about 20 minutes until tender.

meanwhile, mix the garlic and the tomatoes and cook for about 10 minutes, stirring frequently, until the liquid has reduced a little. When the texture is pulpy, add the tomato purée, lemon juice, basil, sugar and seasoning. Heat through and pour over the cooked artichokes in a serving dish. Just before serving, sprinkle with chopped parsley. This dish is equally delicious served hot or cold.

Serves 6
Preparation time: *20 minutes*
Cooking time: *30 minutes*

kcal 90 • KJ 445 • protein 4 g
• fat 0 g • CHO 22 g

Scalloped Potatoes

2 teaspoons vegetable oil
75 ml/3 fl oz low-fat soured cream
350 ml/12 fl oz skimmed milk
25 g/1 oz low-fat spread
1 tablespoon cornflour
⅛ teaspoon pepper
4 medium potatoes, about 750 g/1½ lb, cut into 5 mm/¼ inch slices
½ medium onion, diced
paprika, to taste
sprigs of thyme, to serve

brush a rectangular 20 cm/8 inch x 12 cm/5 inch baking dish with oil.

in a medium bowl, whisk together the soured cream, skimmed milk, low-fat spread, cornflour and pepper.

line the dish with one-third of the potato slices. Pour one-third of the soured cream mixture over the potatoes. Sprinkle half of the onion over the soured cream mixture. Repeat the layers in order: one-third of the potatoes, one-third of the soured cream mixture and the remaining onion. Arrange the remaining potatoes on the top and pour the remaining soured cream mixture over the top. Cover with foil and bake in a preheated oven at 180°C/350°F/Gas Mark 4 for 1 hour. Remove the foil and bake for a further 20 minutes.

sprinkle with paprika and thyme sprigs, then let stand for 5 minutes before serving.

Serves 6
Preparation time: *20 minutes*
Cooking time: *1 hour 20 minutes*
Oven temperature:
  180°C/350°F/Gas Mark 4

Kcal 185 • KJ 777 • protein 5 g
• fat 5 g.• CHO 30 g

Pan-braised Peppers *with Tomato*

This delicious dish, full of flavour and colour, is suitable for vegetarians.

1 tablespoon vegetable oil
2 medium onions, coarsely chopped
3 large peppers, red, green and yellow, total weight about 500 g/1 lb, cored, deseeded and cut into strips
500 g/1 lb tomatoes, skinned and chopped
1 teaspoon coriander seeds
1 teaspoon black peppercorns
½ teaspoon salt
½ teaspoon ground chilli

heat the oil in a large frying pan and fry the onions for about 5 minutes until golden. Add the peppers and cook gently for 2–3 minutes, then stir in the tomatoes.

crush the coriander seeds and peppercorns. Use a pestle and mortar if you have one, otherwise put the seeds and peppercorns between double sheets of kitchen paper and crush with a rolling pin. Add the salt and chilli to the crushed seeds and sprinkle the mixture over the peppers and tomatoes. Mix together lightly, cover the pan and cook gently for 20 minutes. This can be prepared up to 24 hours in advance and kept covered in the refrigerator.

Serves 4
Preparation time: *25 minutes*
Cooking time: *28 minutes*

kcal 96 • KJ 407 • protein 3 g • fat 4 g • CHO 14 g

clipboard: It is not essential to use different-coloured peppers, but it does look attractive. This dish is wonderful served hot and almost as good served cold with a salad selection.

Raw Vegetables
with Yellow Bean Sauce

Good vegetables to choose for this dish are peeled broccoli stalks, carrot, cucumber and courgette sticks, French beans, Chinese leaves, cauliflower florets and strips of red and yellow pepper.

about 500 g/1 lb vegetables of your choice
1 large fresh red chilli, sliced lengthways, to garnish

Sauce
125 g/4 oz yellow bean sauce
½ onion, chopped
1 tablespoon tamarind water
200 ml/7 fl oz coconut milk
200 ml/7 fl oz water
2 eggs
3 tablespoons sugar
1 tablespoon soy sauce

choose a mixture of raw vegetables and chop them into bite-sized pieces.

make the sauce: blend the yellow bean sauce and the onion in a blender or food processor and turn into a saucepan. Add the rest of the sauce ingredients and bring gradually to the boil, stirring. Remove from the heat and pour into a bowl.

garnish the sauce with the sliced chilli and serve warm, with the vegetables.

Serves 4 as a vegetarian main course
Preparation time: *15 minutes*
Cooking time: *5–6 minutes*

kcal 152 • KJ 643 • protein 7 g
• fat 4 g • CHO 24 g

clipboard: Tamarind refers to the dried pods of the tamarind, or Indian date. These are sour tasting and need to be soaked in hot water to extract the flavour. Tamarind can be bought as a paste in jars and needs to be mixed with a little water to bring it to a runny consistency. Lemon is often used as a substitute, though tamarind has a much stronger flavour.

Summer Vegetables
with Yogurt and Mint

250 g/8 oz broad beans (weighed without pods)
250 g/8 oz runner beans, strings removed and sliced
250 g/8 oz fresh peas (weighed without pods)
150 ml/5 fl oz natural yogurt
1 tablespoon chopped fresh mint
salt and freshly ground black pepper

cook the broad beans for about 8 minutes in a little boiling, salted water, then drain thoroughly.

cook the runner beans and peas together for 5 minutes in boiling water and drain thoroughly.

heat the yogurt very gently in one of the vegetable pans, add the vegetables and toss to coat thoroughly. Gently stir in the black pepper to taste and the mint, and serve.

Serves 4
Preparation time: *25 minutes*
Cooking time: *15 minutes*

kcal 119 • KJ 503 • protein 11 g
• fat 1 g • CHO 17 g

clipboard: Broad beans originated in Persia and Africa, and have been used in European – especially Mediterranean – cuisine for centuries. The beans are shelled and the tough outer skin may be removed before cooking.

Vegetables

Pumpkin

Carrots

Celeriac

Jerusalem artichokes

Jerusalem artichokes

This is a native American vegetable, which is not in fact an artichoke at all but a tuber of a species of sunflower. The word Jerusalem is probably, in fact, derived from *girasole*, which is Italian for sunflower. Jerusalem artichokes can be eaten raw in salads, or cooked like potatoes as an accompanying vegetable. They make a particularly delicious soup.

Carrots

Long root vegetables with sweet orange flesh, carrots are highly nutritious, particularly when they are eaten raw. They can also be cooked in casseroles or served as an accompanying vegetable.

Celeriac

Grown for its swollen, knobbly root, celeriac has a firm, crisp white flesh, and a flavour similar to that of celery. It may be eaten raw in salads, or cooked in soups, stews and casseroles. It is at its best in winter.

Pumpkin

The pumpkin is a member of the gourd family. It has a slightly bland flesh, but is delicious in well-flavoured soups and pies.

Celery

Sweet peppers

Shiitake mushrooms

Oyster mushrooms

Red cabbage

Red cabbage

Cabbage – both green and red – is a highly nutritious vegetable with tightly packed leaves. It can be served as an accompanying vegetable with meat or fish, or eaten raw in salads. Red cabbage is available all year round and is relatively inexpensive.

Celery

A long crisp stalk, celery is most commonly used either in salads, when it gives a welcome crunchiness, or it can be cooked as an accompanying vegetable or in soups, casseroles and stews. It is available all year round and is relatively inexpensive.

Sweet peppers

Green, red and yellow peppers can be used to add colour and texture to salads, or cooked in soups, stews and stir-fries. They are especially rich in vitamin C.

Mushrooms

Possibly one of the oldest plants in the world, mushrooms are available all year round. There are some 250 different varieties of edible fungus, including oyster and shiitake mushrooms. Shiitake mushrooms have a fragrant, golden brown cap, which is often dried in China as this makes their flavour even more pronounced.

Grilled Courgettes
with Mustard

500 g/1 lb courgettes, cut in half lengthways
15 g/½ oz butter or soya margarine, melted
1 tablespoon wholegrain mustard

brush the courgettes lightly with the melted butter and place them, cut-side down, on a heated grill pan or griddle pan. Grill under high heat until lightly browned.

turn them over and spread with the mustard. Grill until golden. Serve hot as a starter or an accompanying vegetable.

Serves 4
Preparation time: *10 minutes*
Cooking time: *10 minutes*

kcal 60 • KJ 252 • protein 2 g • fat 4 g • CHO 5 g

clipboard: Soya margarine can be used instead of butter or vegetable margarine for all dishes. It is suitable for vegans and is a healthy option because it is particularly low in saturated fats.

Broccoli Dressed
with Lemon

1 kg/2 lb fresh broccoli
1 teaspoon olive oil
2 very thin strips of lemon rind, about
4 cm/1½ inches long
2 tablespoons lemon juice
generous pinch of grated nutmeg
salt and freshly ground black pepper

trim most of the stalk off the broccoli heads. Peel the stalks and slice them thinly, diagonally. Wash the heads and break into small florets.

steam the broccoli heads for 8 minutes, then taste to see if they are done; they should still have some bite.

while the heads are steaming, cook the stalks. Heat the oil in a wok or large frying pan until very hot, add the lemon rind and fry it until it starts to brown, then quickly add the sliced stalks. Stir-fry for barely 1 minute, then add the lemon juice, nutmeg and salt and pepper to taste, and fry for a further 30 seconds.

place the steamed florets in a serving dish and lay the stalks on top. Stir once, then leave to cool a little.

serve while still warm.

Serves 6
Preparation time: *20 minutes*
Cooking time: *10 minutes, plus standing time*

kcal 54 • KJ 235 • protein 7 g • fat 2 g • CHO 3 g

clipboard: Nutmeg is the seed of the nutmeg tree and is dried in the sun after harvesting. It is sold either whole or ground, and is better bought whole and freshly grated, as the ground form quickly loses its spicy aroma.

Root Vegetable Bake

500 g/1 lb new potatoes, washed
250 g/8 oz swedes, peeled and cubed
300 g/10 oz parsnips, peeled and sliced
250 g/8 oz carrots, peeled and cut into sticks
65 ml/2½ fl oz Vegetable Stock (see page 244)
50 g/2 oz reduced-fat cheese, preferably Edam or
Cheddar, grated
salt and freshly ground black pepper

Garnish
tomato slices
1 tablespoon chopped fresh parsley (optional)

preheat the oven to 180°C/350°F/Gas Mark 4.

place the potatoes in a pan of boiling salted water and cook until just tender. Cut into 5 mm/¼ inch slices. Place the remaining vegetables together in a large pan of salted water and bring to the boil. Boil until just tender. Drain all the vegetables and place in layers in a deep ovenproof dish, finishing with a border of overlapping potato slices. Pour over the stock, sprinkle with the cheese and season with pepper.

bake in the oven for 15–20 minutes or until the cheese has melted and the vegetables are heated through. Brown under a moderate grill to finish, if wished.

serve garnished with tomato slices and chopped parsley if using.

Serves 4
Preparation time: *20 minutes*
Cooking time: *about 40–50 minutes*

*kcal 185 • KJ 780 • protein 8 g
• fat 3 g • CHO 34 g*

clipboard: An alternative is to cover the top completely with potato slices. Diced grilled bacon may be added before baking, but this will, of course, add to the fat content.

Pumpkin Curry

50 g/2 oz fresh coconut, grated

300 ml/½ pint coconut water (from a fresh coconut)

2 tablespoons vegetable oil

I onion, chopped

I green pepper, cored, deseeded and chopped

4 garlic cloves, crushed

2 slices fresh root ginger, peeled and finely chopped

¼ teaspoon turmeric

2 fresh green chillies, deseeded and finely chopped

¼ teaspoon ground cloves

¼ teaspoon crushed chilli flakes

750 g/1½ lb pumpkin, peeled, deseeded and cut into 2.5 cm/1 inch cubes

2 tomatoes, skinned and chopped

salt and freshly ground black pepper

put the grated fresh coconut in a bowl and add the coconut water. You can drain this out of a fresh coconut by piercing it a couple of times with a skewer and draining out the liquid. (If you don't get enough water out of your coconut, simply make up the quantity with water.) Leave the coconut to soak for about 30 minutes.

heat the vegetable oil in a large, heavy saucepan and add the onion, green pepper and garlic. Fry gently over a very low heat, stirring occasionally, until the onion and pepper are softened and golden brown.

add the fresh root ginger, turmeric, chillies, cloves and chilli flakes to the onion and pepper mixture. Stir well and continue cooking over low heat for 2–3 minutes, stirring.

add the pumpkin, tomatoes and the coconut and coconut water. Bring to the boil and then reduce the heat to a bare simmer. Cover the pan and cook gently for 20 minutes, until the pumpkin is tender but not mushy. Season to taste with salt and pepper and serve hot.

Serves 6
Preparation time: *20 minutes, plus soaking*
Cooking time: *30–35 minutes*

kcal 87 • KJ 364 • protein 2 g • fat 5 g • CHO 8 g

clipboard: Cloves are the immature flower buds of an evergreen tree from southeast Asia, east Africa and the West Indies. They can be bought either whole or ground, but it is better to buy them whole as ground spices soon lose their aroma.

Caponata

This Sicilian dish is often served as a cold hors d'oeuvre. Pine nuts would be a tasty addition but will increase the fat content.

3 aubergines cut into 1.25 cm/½ inch dice
2 tablespoons olive oil
1 onion, thinly sliced
2 celery sticks, diced
150 ml/¼ pint passata
3 tablespoons wine vinegar
1 yellow pepper, cored, deseeded and finely sliced
1 red pepper, cored, deseeded and finely sliced
25 g/1 oz anchovy fillets, soaked in warm water, drained and dried
50 g/2 oz capers, roughly chopped
25 g/1 oz black olives, pitted and sliced
25 g/1 oz green olives, pitted and sliced
25 g/1 oz pine nuts (optional)
salt
2 tablespoons chopped parsley, to serve

put the diced aubergines into a colander, sprinkle with salt and leave to drain for 15–20 minutes to exude their bitter juices. Rinse under running cold water to remove any salt and pat dry with kitchen paper.

heat the oil in a saucepan, add the onion and sauté until soft and golden. Add the celery and cook for 2–3 minutes. Add the aubergine and cook gently for 3 minutes, stirring occasionally. Add the passata and cook gently until it has been absorbed. Spoon in the wine vinegar and cook for 1 minute. Add the peppers, anchovies, capers, olives and pine nuts, if liked, and cook for a further 3 minutes.

transfer the mixture to an ovenproof dish and bake, covered, in a preheated oven at 180°C/350°F/Gas Mark 4 for about 1 hour. Serve lukewarm or cold sprinkled with chopped parsley.

Serves 6
Preparation time: *40 minutes, plus 15–20 minutes daining time*
Cooking time: *1¼ hours*
Oven temperature: *180°C/350°F/ Gas Mark 4*

kcal 74 • KJ 313 • protein 3 g • fat 4 g • CHO 7 g

clipboard: Passata is a convenient way of buying sieved tomatoes and is widely available in bottles and cartons from supermarkets and health food shops.

Spicy Roast Vegetables

These lightly spiced roast vegetables are delicious as a starter or a side dish. Although they are called roast vegetables, they are actually better cooked in a large heavy-based grill pan.

2 tablespoons good-quality extra-virgin olive oil
½ teaspoon white cumin seeds
1 green pepper, cored, deseeded and thickly sliced
1 red pepper, cored, deseeded and thickly sliced
1 orange pepper, cored, deseeded and thickly sliced
2 courgettes, diagonally sliced
2 tomatoes, halved
2 red onions, quartered
1 aubergine, thickly sliced
2 thick fresh green chillies, sliced
4 garlic cloves
1 x 2.5 cm/1 inch piece fresh root ginger, shredded
1 teaspoon dried crushed red chillies
½ teaspoon salt
1 tablespoon chopped fresh coriander, to garnish
lemon wedges, to serve

heat the grill pan for 2 minutes. Pour in the olive oil, then add the cumin seeds. Lower the heat to medium.

arrange the vegetables in the pan with a pair of tongs, then add the green chillies, garlic, ginger, red chillies and salt and increase the heat. Cook the vegetables for 7–10 minutes, turning them with the tongs.

serve hot with lemon wedges and garnish with the fresh coriander.

Serves 6
Preparation time: *10 minutes*
Cooking time: *15 minutes*

kcal 78 • KJ 324 • protein 2 g • fat 4 g • CHO 8 g

Two-Bean Vegetable Goulash

125 g/4 oz each black-eyed and cannellini beans, soaked overnight
1 tablespoon vegetable oil
125 g/4 oz very small onions, or shallots, peeled but left whole
4 sticks of celery, sliced into chunks
4 small courgettes, cut in chunks
3 small carrots, cut in chunks
1 x 400 g/13 oz can tomatoes
300 ml/½ pint Vegetable Stock (see page 244)
1 tablespoon paprika
½ teaspoon caraway seeds
1 tablespoon cornflour
2 tablespoons water
salt and freshly ground black pepper
soured cream, fromage frais or low-fat crème fraîche, to serve (optional)

drain the beans and rinse under cold running water. Put them in two separate pans, cover with water and bring to the boil. Boil fast for 10 minutes, then lower the heat, half-cover the pans and simmer for about 1 hour until tender. Drain, rinse and set aside.

heat the oil in a large pan and fry the onions, celery, courgettes and carrots quickly over a high heat until lightly browned. Pour in the tomatoes with their juice and the stock. Stir in the paprika, caraway seeds, salt and pepper, to taste. Cover and simmer for 20 minutes until the vegetables are tender.

stir both lots of cooked beans into the vegetables. Blend the cornflour with the water and add to the pan. Bring to the boil, stirring, until the sauce thickens a little. Cover the pan and simmer again for about 10 minutes. Spoon the goulash into a warmed dish and serve with a little soured cream, fromage frais or low-fat crème fraîche, if liked.

Serves 4
Preparation time: *30 minutes, plus soaking*
Cooking time: *1 hour 20 minutes*

kcal 238 • KJ 1008 • protein 13 g • fat 4 g • CHO 41 g

clipboard: If you have neither the time nor the inclination to cook dried beans, you can always use canned beans instead.

Noodles with Vegetables

250 g/8 oz low-fat dried egg noodles
2 tablespoons groundnut oil
50 g/2 oz leek, sliced
25 g/1 oz oyster mushrooms, torn
1 celery stick and leaf, chopped
125 g/4 oz Chinese leaves, sliced
25 g/1 oz cauliflower florets
2 tablespoons soy sauce
1½ tablespoons sugar
½ teaspoon salt
1 teaspoon freshly ground black pepper
2 tablespoons crispy garlic
fresh coriander leaves, to garnish

cook the noodles in boiling water for 5–6 minutes. Drain and rinse in cold water to stop further cooking.

heat the oil in a wok or large frying pan over a moderate heat, then add all of the ingredients one by one, including the noodles. Give a quick stir after each addition.

stir-fry for 3–4 minutes, adding a little more oil if necessary. Check the seasoning.

serve at once, garnished with coriander leaves.

Serves 4
Preparation time: *10 minutes*
Cooking time: *8–10 minutes*

kcal 290 • KJ 1230 • protein 10 g • fat 4 g • CHO 58 g

clipboard: To make crispy fried garlic, heat about 300 ml/½ pint groundnut oil in a wok and, when the oil is hot, throw in about 25 g/1 oz of finely chopped garlic and stir for about 40 seconds. Remove with a slotted spoon and drain as much of the oil as possible, then spread the garlic out to dry on kitchen paper. You can store crispy garlic in an airtight container, where it will keep for up to 1 month. Coriander is a member of the carrot family and looks very similar to flat-leaf parsley. All parts of the plant are edible, including the leaves, seeds and flowers.

Stir-Fried Vegetables

These stir-fried vegetables may be served as an accompaniment to meat or fish, or as a vegetarian main course. They are at their best when they are lightly cooked and are still crunchy.

1 tablespoon vegetable oil
125 g/4 oz bamboo shoots, thinly sliced
50 g/2 oz mangetout
125 g/4 oz carrots, thinly sliced
50 g/2 oz broccoli florets
125 g/4 oz fresh bean sprouts, rinsed
1 teaspoon each salt and sugar
1 tablespoon stock or water

heat the oil in a preheated wok or frying pan. Add the bamboo shoots, mangetout, carrots and broccoli florets and stir-fry for about 1 minute.

add the bean sprouts with the salt and sugar. Stir-fry for another minute or so, then add some stock or water if necessary. Do not overcook or the vegetables will lose their crunchiness. Serve hot.

Serves 4
Preparation time: *15–20 minutes*
Cooking time: *3–5 minutes*

kcal 68 • KJ 280 • protein 3 g • fat 3 g • CHO 7 g

clipboard: It is best to use fresh bean sprouts for this dish, in which case you should buy them on the day you plan to use them. Canned bean sprouts do not have the crunchy texture that you need for this recipe.

Fish

Plaice with Lemon Sauce

8 small plaice fillets, about 65 g/2½ oz each, skinned
finely grated rind of ½ lemon
1 tablespoon finely chopped parsley
300 ml/½ pint skimmed milk
salt and freshly ground black pepper
dill sprigs, to garnish

Sauce
350 g/12 oz courgettes
300 ml/½ pint Chicken Stock (see page 244)
grated rind of ½ lemon
1 garlic clove, peeled and chopped

spread out the plaice fillets, skinned sides uppermost. Sprinkle with salt and pepper to taste, lemon rind and parsley, and roll each one up.

for the sauce, chop the courgettes and cook together with the stock, lemon rind and garlic until just tender.

blend the cooked courgettes and their liquid until smooth.

put the rolled plaice fillets into a shallow pan. Add the milk and salt and pepper to taste. Poach the fish gently for about 8–10 minutes until it is just tender, then drain, reserving the liquid. Put on a warm serving dish.

heat the courgette purée in a pan with just enough of the fish cooking liquid to give a fairly thick sauce.

spoon the prepared courgette and lemon sauce around the rolled fish fillets and garnish with dill. Serve with courgettes, thinly sliced.

Serves 4
Preparation time: *25–30 minutes*
Cooking time: *about 15 minutes*

kcal 170 • KJ 720 • protein 28 g
• fat 4 g • CHO 8 g

Monkfish Kebabs

Let your guests cook their own kebabs which you have prepared in advance. In this way, you will not still be slaving over the hot coals while everyone else is enjoying their meal. Remember to light the barbecue well ahead of time.

2 kg/4 lb monkfish, cut into 4 cm/1½ inch cubes

1 teaspoon salt

4 tablespoons white wine

2 tablespoons lemon juice

1 sprig fresh rosemary, needles removed and chopped

1 garlic clove, crushed

3 lemons, cut into small chunks

4 green peppers, cored, deseeded and cut into small rectangles

5 pitta breads, halved and warmed, to serve (optional)

sprinkle the monkfish with salt and pour over the wine and lemon juice. Stir in the rosemary and garlic, cover and marinate for 1 hour.

thread cubes of fish, chunks of lemon and pepper pieces alternately on to 10 skewers. Lay the skewers on a dish, sprinkle some of the marinade over and cover with foil.

when the charcoal is ready for cooking, place the skewers on the barbecue rack and cook for 10 minutes, turning frequently.

serve the kebabs in pockets of warm pitta bread, if liked.

Serves 10
Preparation time: *10 minutes, plus marinating*
Cooking time: *10 minutes*

kcal 225 • KJ 960 • protein 35 g • fat 1 g • CHO 19 g

Fish Kebabs Madras

These kebabs are made with monkfish, which holds its shape well and will not fall apart.

4 tablespoons natural yogurt

3 tablespoons lime juice

I garlic clove, crushed

I teaspoon curry powder

6 drops Tabasco sauce

I thin slice fresh ginger, finely chopped

500 g/I lb monkfish or other firm white fish, cut into 2.5 cm/I inch cubes

12 large peeled prawns

12 shelled mussels

salt and freshly ground black pepper

Garnish

I tablespoon roughly chopped fresh coriander

lime wedges

mix the yogurt with the lime juice, garlic, curry powder, Tabasco, chopped ginger and salt and pepper, to taste.

stir the fish, prawns and mussels lightly into the spiced yogurt mixture; cover and chill for 4 hours.

thread the pieces of fish, prawns and mussels alternately on to 4 kebab skewers. Brush off any excess yogurt mixture.

place the kebabs on a lightly greased baking sheet under a preheated grill. Grill for about 6 minutes until the fish is just tender, brushing with extra yogurt marinade.

arrange the kebabs on a platter, sprinkle with coriander and serve with wedges of lime.

Serves 4

Preparation time: *15 minutes, plus chilling*

Cooking time: *about 6 minutes*

kcal 158 • KJ 670 • protein 31 g • fat 2 g • CHO 4 g

Cod Niçoise

This colourful fish dish, with tomatoes, pepper and black olives, brings a flavour of the sunny Mediterranean to your cuisine.

4 x 250 g/8 oz cod fillets, skinned
150 ml/¼ pint dry white wine
150 ml/¼ pint water
slice of onion
bouquet garni
1 clove garlic, crushed
25 g/1 oz low-fat spread
25 g/1 oz plain white flour
150 ml/¼ pint skimmed milk
2 large tomatoes, skinned, seeded and diced
1 pepper, cored, deseeded and finely chopped
salt and pepper

Garnish
12 black olives, pitted
parsley sprigs

heat the oven to 180°C/350°F/Gas Mark 4. Rinse and dry the cod, lay it in an ovenproof dish, add salt and pepper to taste. Pour over the wine and water, adding the onion, bouquet garni and garlic. Cover with oiled greaseproof paper and poach in the oven for 20 minutes. Drain and reserve the liquid. Keep the fish hot.

melt the low-fat spread, stir in the flour and cook for 1 minute. Remove from the heat and gradually stir in 300 ml/½ pint of the fish liquid and the milk. Return to the heat and bring to the boil, stirring, until thick and smooth. Simmer for 2–3 minutes, taste and adjust seasoning. Add the tomatoes and pepper and reheat to boiling. Pour over the fish. Garnish with olives and parsley. Serve with rice.

Serves 4
Preparation time: *15 minutes*
Cooking time: *24 minutes*
Oven temperature:
  180°C/350°F/Gas Mark 4

*kcal 274 • KJ 1158 • protein 42 g
• fat 5 g • CHO 9 g*

Haddock and Cider Casserole

25 g/1 oz low-fat spread
1 medium onion, sliced
40 g/1½ oz plain flour
300 ml/½ pint dry cider
2 leeks, trimmed and sliced
375 g/12 oz cooking apples, peeled, cored and sliced
750 g/1½ lb haddock fillets, skinned and thickly sliced
salt and pepper

Garnish

1 teaspoon oil, to grill the apple rings
1 apple, peeled, cored and sliced
1 tablespoon chopped parsley

heat the oven to 180°C/350°F/Gas Mark 4.

melt the low-fat spread in a saucepan and cook the onion over a moderate heat for 10 minutes, without browning. Stir in the flour and cook for 2 minutes.

add the cider, bring to the boil and cook for 3 minutes, stirring until thickened. Season well.

place the leeks, apple slices and fish in a shallow 1.8 litre/3 pint ovenproof dish. Pour over the sauce. Cover and cook in the oven for 50–60 minutes.

meanwhile, prepare the garnish. Lightly brush the apple rings with oil and grill them until light golden brown on both sides. Remove from the heat and drain on absorbent kitchen paper.

uncover the casserole at the end of the cooking time, and garnish with the grilled apple rings and parsley. Serve immediately.

Serves 4
Preparation time: *30 minutes*
Cooking time: *1 hour 5 minutes–1 hour 15 minutes*
Oven temperature: *180°C/350°F/Gas Mark 4*

kcal 264 • KJ 1110 • protein 32 g • fat 5 g • CHO 20 g

Fish and seafood

Plaice

Prawns

Haddock fillet

Sea bass

Prawns

Prawns are shellfish which are usually sold already cooked and should be bright pink or red in colour. They can be bought either fresh, frozen or canned and are particularly good either grilled or in made-up dishes, hot or cold.

Haddock fillet

Haddock is a sea fish of the cod family and is similarly low in fat and versatile. It is available all year round, though it is best between October and January. It can be bought whole or in fillets, fresh or frozen, and is also available smoked.

Sea bass

Sea bass is a large, stripy fish with a very big head. It is not a common fish and is therefore fairly expensive. It is best between January and March, and then again between August and December. It is good baked, roasted or grilled.

Plaice

Plaice is one of the most popular flat fish and has a mild flavour. It is plentiful all year round, though it is best between June and December. It can be bought either whole or filleted and can be cooked in a great number of different ways.

Sea bream

Rainbow trout

Monkfish tail

Cod fillet

Sea bream

Sea bream is a thick flat fish, with firm, delicately flavoured, white flesh. It is available mainly in the Mediterranean and is best from June to December. It is sold either whole or in fillets and is good stuffed and baked, grilled or poached.

Rainbow trout

Trout is a popular freshwater fish. Farmed trout is available all year round, while river trout, which is still more highly thought of, is available between March and September. It is an oily fish and is therefore relatively high in fat.

Monkfish tail

Monkfish, also known as angler fish, is a large, ugly-looking fish with an enormous head, and is actually a ray-like shark. It is a relatively expensive fish and is available all year round. It is an important ingredient in bouillabaisse and other fish soups, and can be fried, baked or barbecued as kebabs. When it is deep-fried, it is similar to scampi. It contains almost no fat.

Cod fillet

Cod is one of the most versatile and popular white fish. It is a fairly inexpensive fish and has a coarse, flaky flesh and a mild flavour. Like several of the white fish, cod is especially low in fat and is therefore a good choice on a low fat diet. It is plentiful all year round as fillets or steaks, fresh or frozen, and can also be bought smoked or salted.

Sea Bass Baked in Spinach

1 sea bass, weighing about 750 g/1½ lb, cleaned and gutted
275 g/9 oz spinach
2 shallots, chopped
150 ml/¼ pint dry white wine

Stuffing

50 g/2 oz fresh breadcrumbs
15 g/½ oz low-fat spread, melted
2 tablespoons chopped chervil
1 tablespoon chopped tarragon
1 tablespoon chopped basil
1 tablespoon lemon juice
salt and pepper

Garnish

3 orange slices, quartered
small sprigs of tarragon

mix together all the stuffing ingredients, season with salt and pepper to taste, and stuff the fish cavity.

put the spinach in a colander in a bowl and pour over boiling water. Drain thoroughly. Wrap the stuffed sea bass in the blanched spinach, leaving the head and tail exposed. Sprinkle the shallots over the base of a gratin dish and place the fish on top. Pour over the wine. Cover with foil and cook in a preheated oven at 200°C/400°F/Gas Mark 6 for 30 minutes.

transfer to a warmed serving dish and garnish with quartered orange slices and little sprigs of tarragon.

Serves 6
Preparation time: *30 minutes*
Cooking time: *30 minutes*
Oven temperature:
   200°C/400°F/Gas Mark 6

kcal 189 • KJ 795 • protein 27 g • fat 5 g • CHO 7 g

clipboard: Sea bass is a marine fish caught primarily off the Provençal coast and known in France as *loup*, meaning wolf, presumably because it is such a fierce predator. It is in quite short supply and is therefore an expensive fish but is worth the price because of its delicate flavour. It should be really fresh. In choosing it, you should look for firmness of flesh, brightness of eye and gleaming skin with its beautiful markings.

Sweet and Sour Cod Cutlets

4 individual cod cutlets or steaks
15 g/½ oz sunflower margarine
1 onion, thinly sliced
150 ml/¼ pint Fish or Vegetable Stock (see pages 244–245)
150 ml/¼ pint orange juice
2 tablespoons wine vinegar
1 tablespoon soy sauce
2 teaspoons soft brown sugar
1½ tablespoons cornflour

Garnish
julienne strips of orange rind, blanched
spring onions

place the pieces of cod in a pan large enough to hold them in a single layer. Cover with cold water and bring slowly to the boil over a moderate heat. Poach gently for about 10 minutes or until the fish is tender.

meanwhile, melt the margarine in a pan and sauté the onion for 5–7 minutes, until soft but not brown. Add the stock, orange juice, vinegar, soy sauce and sugar to the pan and stir well to combine.

blend the cornflour with a little water in a small bowl to make a creamy paste and add to the sauce. Bring to the boil, stirring, until the sauce is thickened. Simmer for 3–5 minutes.

when the fish is cooked, lift the cod portions out of the pan with a slotted spoon and place in a serving dish. Pour the sauce over the fish. To serve, garnish with strips of orange rind and spring onions.

Serves 4
Preparation time: *15 minutes*
Cooking time: *10 minutes*

kcal 256 • KJ 1081 • protein 36 g • fat 5 g • CHO 18 g

clipboard: Use any other white fish that you have available such as haddock or whiting, fresh or frozen. If you like, fine strips of green, red or yellow pepper can be added to the sauce. Serve with mashed potatoes and a seasonal green vegetable .

Portuguese Cod

Cook cod fillets in the Portuguese style to make them more interesting.

1 onion, chopped
25 g/1 oz low-fat spread
1 clove garlic, crushed
4 tomatoes, skinned and chopped
juice of 1 lemon
4 x 200 g/7 oz cod fillets
salt and freshly ground black pepper
chopped parsley, to garnish

soften the chopped onion in the low-fat spread over medium heat, without allowing it to brown. Add the crushed garlic, chopped tomatoes and lemon juice. Season to taste with salt and freshly ground black pepper and stir well.

spoon about one-third of this sauce into a shallow ovenproof dish. Arrange the cod fillets on top, then pour over the remaining sauce. Cover the dish with a lid or with aluminium foil and bake in a moderately hot oven at 190°C/375°F/Gas Mark 5 for 25–30 minutes.

remove from the oven and sprinkle over a little chopped parsley to garnish before serving.

Serves 4
Preparation time: *15 minutes*
Cooking time: *25–30 minutes*

kcal 197 • KJ 833 • protein 36 g
• fat 4 g • CHO 4 g

clipboard: Cod is particularly low in fat. It has a moist, firm, creamy-white flesh, which flakes when it is cooked. It is extremely versatile and can be prepared in many different ways. However, prolonged cooking harms both the flavour and the presentation.

Fillet of Sole
with Melon and Mint

4 fillets of sole, halved

2 tablespoons chopped mint

300 ml/½ pint dry white wine

I Charentais melon, halved and deseeded

150 ml/¼ pint natural yogurt

salt and pepper

sprigs of fresh mint, to garnish

season the sole fillets with salt and pepper and sprinkle with half of the mint. Roll up each fish fillet and secure with wooden cocktail sticks. Place the fish rolls in a deep frying pan and sprinkle over the remaining mint. Add the white wine. Cover the pan and poach gently for about 8 minutes, until the fish is tender.

meanwhile, using a Parisian cutter or melon ball cutter, scoop the melon flesh into small balls. Cut out any remaining melon flesh attached to the skin.

carefully drain the rolled fillets, place on a warm serving dish and keep warm. Remove the cocktail sticks.

boil the poaching liquid with the remnants of melon flesh until well reduced and whisk until smooth. If necessary, purée in a food processor or blender.

stir in the yogurt and heat the sauce through gently. Season with salt and pepper and spoon over the cooked fish. Garnish with the melon balls and sprigs of mint.

Serves 4
Preparation time: *20 minutes*
Cooking time: *10–12 minutes*

Kcal 230 • KJ 985 • protein 29 g
• fat 3 g • CHO 12 g

Tarragon-infused Sea Bass

4 x 175 g/6 oz sea bass fillets
large bunch of tarragon
1 teaspoon olive oil
juice of 1 lemon
sea salt flakes and pepper
lemon wedges, to serve

heat a grill or griddle pan, put on the sea bass, skin side down, and cook for 3 minutes. Place a quarter of the tarragon on each fillet, pressing it into the fish.

turn the fish so that it is resting on the tarragon and cook for a further 3 minutes.

drizzle over the olive oil and lemon juice, and season. Serve with the charred tarragon and lemon wedges.

Serves 4
Preparation time: *5 minutes*
Cooking time: *6 minutes*

Kcal 184 • KJ 774 • protein 34 g • fat 5 g • CHO 1 g

Plaice with Mushrooms and Cider

8 x 50 g/2 oz fresh or frozen plaice fillets
450 ml/¾ pint dry cider
500 g/1 lb button mushrooms
2 tablespoons Fish Stock (see page 245)
2 tablespoons flour
500 g/1 lb potatoes, cooked
skimmed milk
2 tablespoons chopped parsley
salt and white pepper

allow the fish fillets, if they are frozen, to thaw to room temperature. Season with salt and pepper, fold up each into three and lay in a sauté pan. Pour in the cider. Bring slowly to the boil, cover and cook for 10 minutes over a very gentle heat.

meanwhile, slice the mushrooms and cook in the stock until just soft. Sprinkle on the flour and mix in carefully until it is absorbed. Strain the cider liquor from the fish into a bowl and then add it slowly to the mushrooms, stirring. Cook for a few minutes, stirring constantly, until the sauce thickens.

arrange the plaice fillets on a hot serving dish and pour over the mushroom and cider sauce. Cream the potatoes with a little skimmed milk, seasoning and the chopped parsley. Serve with a watercress and orange salad, if liked.

Serves 4
Preparation time: *15 minutes*
Cooking time: *20 minutes*

kcal 292 • KJ 1235 • protein 24 g
• fat 4 g • CHO 35 g

Fish Pie

*This is a wholesome and popular family dish.
Serve it with green peas or a salad, either of which
would add a touch of colour.*

750 g/1½ lb cod or haddock fillets, or a mixture
of white fish
about 300 ml/½ pint skimmed milk
bay leaf
½ onion, sliced
6 peppercorns
25 g/1 oz butter or margarine
3 tablespoons flour
2 tablespoons chopped parsley or dill
4 tomatoes, peeled and sliced
1 kg/2 lb potatoes
150 ml/¼ pint hot skimmed milk
salt and white pepper

simmer the fish gently in skimmed milk and water to cover, with the bay leaf, onion and peppercorns, until cooked. Measure off the fish liquor and make up to 450 ml/¾ pint with more skimmed milk if necessary.

melt the butter or margarine and stir in the flour. Cook over a gentle heat for 1 minute, then stir in the strained fish liquor. Bring to the boil, stirring, until the sauce is smooth and thick. Season to taste and stir in the chopped parsley or dill. Pour a little sauce into a greased ovenproof dish and lay the fish on top of it. Top with the tomato slices and cover with the remaining sauce.

meanwhile, cook the potatoes and beat to a purée with the hot skimmed milk. Season and pile on top of the fish mixture. Brown under the grill for a few minutes before serving, if liked.

Serves 6
Preparation time: *10 minutes*
Cooking time: *15 minutes*

*kcal 327 • KJ 1383 • protein 27 g
• fat 5 g • CHO 46 g*

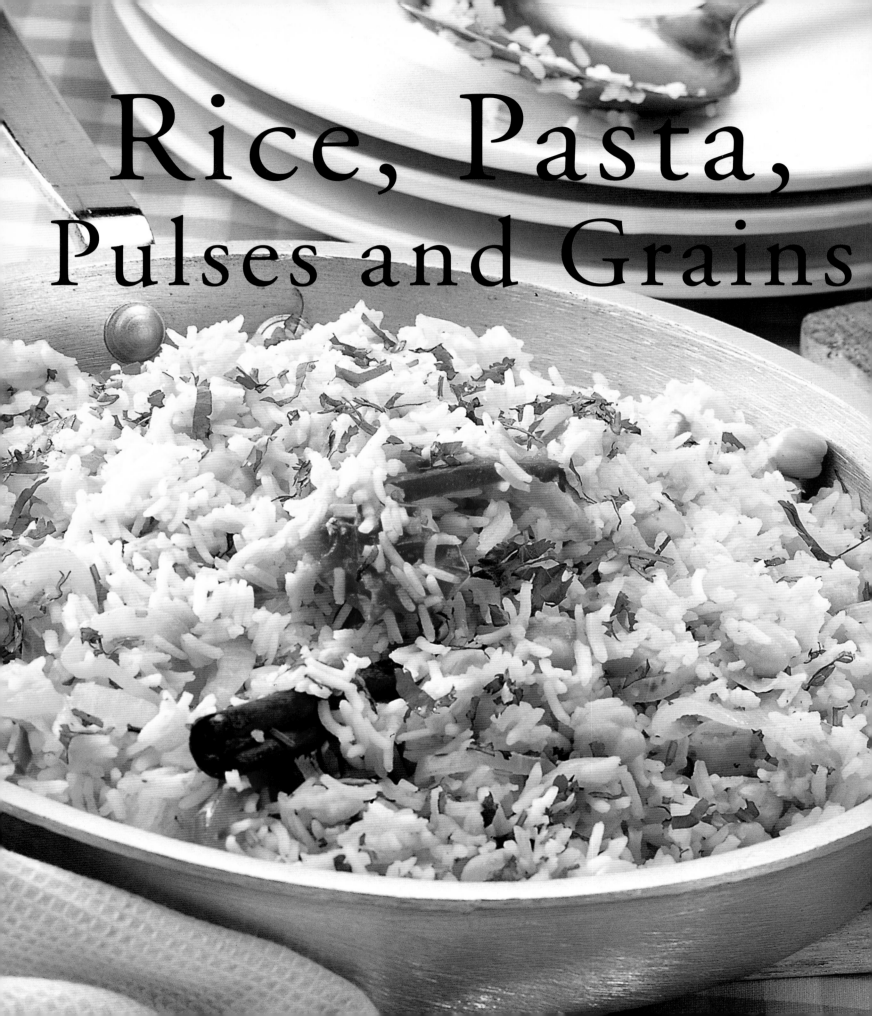

Rice, Pasta, Pulses and Grains

Jamaican Rice
and Peas

250 g/8 oz dried red kidney beans
600 ml/1 pint coconut milk
2 sprigs of fresh thyme, finely chopped
2 spring onions, finely chopped
1 fresh green chilli, deseeded and finely chopped
500 g/1 lb long-grain rice
salt and freshly ground black pepper

put the dried red kidney beans in a large bowl and cover with cold water. Leave to soak overnight. The following day, rinse the kidney beans and drain well.

put the kidney beans in a large saucepan and add 900 ml/1½ pints boiling water. Cook for about 30 minutes, until the kidney beans are almost tender.

add the coconut milk, thyme, spring onions and chilli to the saucepan. Season with salt and pepper and bring back to boiling point. Boil rapidly for 5 minutes.

add the rice and stir well. Cover and simmer gently over low heat until the rice is tender and all the liquid has been absorbed. This will take about 20–25 minutes. If there is any remaining liquid, drain the rice and 'peas' (kidney beans). Transfer to a serving dish and serve hot.

Serves 6
Preparation time: *5 minutes, plus soaking*
Cooking time: *55 minutes*

kcal 434 • KJ 1829 • protein 16 g • fat 1 g • CHO 90 g

clipboard: It may be more convenient and quicker to use canned kidney beans rather than dried ones.

Rice Pilaf

One of the simplest ways of cooking rice, this is probably also one of the most delicious.

250 g/8 oz long-grain rice
I onion, chopped
a little Chicken or Vegetable Stock (see page 244)
I teaspoon ground turmeric
I tablespoon currants
I x 250 g/8 oz can pineapple pieces, drained
salt

cook the rice in boiling salted water for 10 minutes or according to packet instructions. Drain and sprinkle with a little cold water in order to separate the grains. Keep warm in a covered dish.

cook the onion in a little stock and add the turmeric, currants and pineapple pieces. Drain. Toss the rice in this mixture and serve.

Serves 4
Preparation time: *15 minutes*
Cooking time: *20 minutes*

kcal 253 • KJ 1063 • protein 5 g • fat 5 g • CHO 58 g

clipboard: Turmeric comes from the same family as ginger, and in the East it is often used fresh like ginger. It has bright orange flesh which turns yellow when dried. It is also available dried, either whole or ground, and is probably best bought ground because it is so hard, but should be bought often and in small quantities as it soon begins to taste musty. It is often used as a cheaper alternative to saffron, which is such an expensive spice. It is also used as a dye, most famously in the yellow robes of Buddhist monks, and you should be careful when using it in the kitchen as it can stain clothes and work surfaces.

Mussel Risotto

1 kg/2 lb mussels in their shells
1 teaspoon oil
1 small onion, roughly chopped
1 garlic clove, roughly chopped
150 ml/¼ pint Fish Stock (see page 245)
or white wine

Risotto:

1 tablespoon olive oil
2 small onions, peeled and finely chopped
1–2 garlic cloves, finely chopped
375 g/12 oz arborio rice
1 litre/1¾ pints Fish Stock (see page 245)
salt and freshly ground black pepper

wash the mussels in plenty of cold water, discarding any that do not close when tapped sharply. Heat the oil in a large pan, add the onion and garlic and cook for several minutes. Add the fish stock or white wine and the mussels. Heat briskly until the mussels open. Strain and reserve the cooking liquid, and remove the fish from both their shells. Do not try to force open any mussels whose shells do not open properly – simply discard them.

make the risotto: heat the oil and cook the onions and garlic gently for 5 minutes. Add the rice and stir over a low heat. Meanwhile, heat the fish stock. Add the reserved liquid from opening the mussels, plus enough hot fish stock to cover the rice. Cook steadily until the rice has absorbed the liquid, then add a little seasoning and spoon over more of the stock. Continue adding liquid until the rice is almost tender, then gently stir in the shelled mussels, reserving a few in their shells to garnish, and enough of the hot stock needed to produce the correct texture. Adjust the seasoning and heat for the last few minutes. Serve with a sprinkling of grated low-fat or reduced-fat cheese, if liked.

Serves 4
Preparation time: *30 minutes*
Cooking time: *20 minutes*

Kcal 419 • KJ 1757 • protein 20 g
• fat 5 g • CHO 73 g

clipboard: A risotto should have a soft, creamy texture, which is achieved by using the right kind of rice and adding the liquid gradually during the cooking process. Instead of arborio rice, you can use short-grain – the type that is used to make milk puddings. To enjoy a risotto at its best, it should be served immediately after cooking.

Yellow Rice with Mushrooms

1 tablespoon groundnut oil
500 g/1 lb cold cooked rice
125 g/4 oz mangetout, topped and tailed
125 g/4 oz button mushrooms, halved
125 g/4 oz bamboo shoots
1 teaspoon turmeric
2 teaspoons sugar
1 tablespoon soy sauce
1 teaspoon salt
ground black pepper, to taste

Garnish
1 tablespoon crispy fried garlic (see clipboard)
1 large fresh red chilli, deseeded and cut into strips

heat the oil in a wok. Add the rice and give it a good stir, then add the rest of the ingredients. Stir-fry over a low heat until thoroughly mixed. Increase the heat and stir for 1–2 minutes, making sure that the rice does not stick to the wok.

turn on to a serving dish, garnish with the crispy garlic and chilli and serve at once.

Serves 4
Preparation time: *3 minutes*
Cooking time: *3–4 minutes*

Kcal 212 • KJ 896 • protein 6 g • fat 4 g • CHO 42 g

clipboard: Bamboo shoots are part of the bamboo plant, which grows all over tropical Asia. The shoots have been used in Chinese cooking for centuries. They are sweet and crunchy, and can be bought either fresh or canned, though the fresh ones are crunchier then the canned ones. To make crispy fried garlic, heat about 300 ml/½ pint groundnut oil in a wok and, when the oil is hot, throw in about 25 g/1 oz of finely chopped garlic and stir for about 40 seconds. Remove with a slotted spoon and drain as much of the oil as possible, then spread the garlic out to dry on kitchen paper. You can store crispy garlic in an airtight container, where it will keep for up to 1 month.

Chick Pea and Tomato Rice

This is a versatile, lightly flavoured rice. Use a good-quality Basmati rice, soak it for 20–30 minutes, then drain well. The lid of the saucepan must fit well to ensure perfect rice.

1 tablespoon vegetable ghee or butter
1 teaspoon corn oil
2 onions, sliced
2 black cardamoms
1 cinnamon stick
2 whole cloves
4 black peppercorns
1 teaspoon ginger pulp
1 teaspoon garlic pulp
1½ teaspoons salt
2 tomatoes, sliced
1 x 425 g/14 oz can chick peas, drained
400 g/13 oz Basmati rice, washed and drained
2 tablespoons chopped fresh coriander
750 ml/1¼ pints water

heat the ghee or butter with the oil in a saucepan until hot.

add the onions, black cardamoms, cinnamon, cloves and peppercorns and stir-fry over a high heat for about 2 minutes, then add the ginger, garlic, salt and sliced tomatoes.

stir in the drained chick peas and rice and lower the heat to medium. Add 1 tablespoon of the fresh coriander.

pour in the water, cover tightly and cook for about 15–20 minutes or until all the water has been fully absorbed.

remove from the heat and leave to stand for 3–5 minutes before serving the rice, garnished with the remaining fresh coriander.

Serves 6
Preparation time: *15 minutes, including standing*
Cooking time: *15–20 minutes*

Kcal 349 • KJ 1464 • protein 10 g • fat 5 g • CHO 67 g

Mushroom Risotto

Mushroom risotto is a classic Italian dish and an all-time favourite. It requires a lot of stirring, but is well worth the effort for its deliciously creamy texture.

15g/½ oz low-fat spread
1 onion, sliced
250 g/8 oz medium-grain brown rice
150 ml/¼ pint dry white wine
600 ml/1 pint boiling Vegetable or Chicken Stock (see page 244), kept simmering
250 g/8 oz mushrooms, sliced
1 tablespoon fresh basil
1 tablespoon freshly grated Parmesan cheese
salt and freshly ground black pepper

melt the low-fat spread in a saucepan, and fry the onion until golden. Stir in the rice, and cook for 5 minutes, stirring frequently.

add the wine and bring to the boil. Continue boiling until well reduced. Stir in a ladleful of the stock, the mushrooms, basil and seasoning to taste. Simmer, stirring, until all the liquid has been absorbed.

continue simmering, gradually stirring in all of the stock until the liquid has been absorbed.

stir in the grated Parmesan, and serve immediately.

Serves 4
Preparation time: *30 minutes*
Cooking time: *about 20 minutes*

Kcal 272 • KJ 1152 • protein 7 g • fat 5 g • CHO 48 g

Kedgeree

A traditional English breakfast dish, this is absolutely perfect for a leisurely Sunday treat when you have a little more time on your hands, or if you have overnight guests.

500 g/1 lb smoked haddock, soaked in cold water
1 small onion, finely chopped
2 tablespoons Fish or Vegetable Stock
(see pages 244–245)
½ teaspoon curry powder
250 g/8 oz long-grain rice
bay leaf
juice of 1 lemon
3 tablespoons chopped parsley
salt and freshly ground black pepper
lemon wedges, to serve

bring the haddock barely to the boil in fresh water and simmer for a few minutes until tender. Drain and flake. Cook the onion in the stock until soft, then sprinkle over the curry powder and cook for 1 minute longer.

meanwhile, cook the rice in plenty of boiling salted water, with the bay leaf, for 10 minutes. Drain and sprinkle over a few drops of cold water to separate the grains and stop the rice from further cooking.

combine the flaked haddock, the onion mixture and the rice. Grind plenty of black pepper into the kedgeree and sprinkle over the lemon juice and parsley. Toss lightly and pile into a hot dish.

serve with lemon wedges.

Serves 4
Preparation time: *25 minutes*
Cooking time: *about 20 minutes*

Kcal 326 • KJ 1370 • protein 31 g
• fat 1 g • CHO 47 g

Noodles, rice and pasta

Rice noodles

Brown rice

Long-grain rice

Risotto rice

Rice noodles

Rice noodles are made from rice flour. Dried rice noodles are as fine as string and are widely used in Oriental cooking. They may be boiled or deep fried quickly in hot oil. Some specialist Oriental shops also sell fresh rice noodles, which are smooth, flimsy and have a very bland flavour.

Brown rice

Brown rice has been subjected to the absolute minimum of processing. The tough hull has been removed but the outer bran has been left intact. This means that it is a lot more nutritious than polished, or white, rice. It takes rather longer to cook. It is often used in vegetarian diets.

Long-grain rice

Long-grain rice is about four to five times as long as it is wide, with tapered ends. The cooked grains are dry, separate and fluffy. It is the rice that is used in the great majority of savoury rice dishes, including the boiled or steamed rice that is served with curries, pilafs and salads.

Risotto rice

Properly called arborio rice, this is a short-grain rice which is grown in the Po Valley of Italy. It has a particularly high starch content, which is the reason that risotto is renowned for its rich, creamy texture. It can also be used in soups and to make rice puddings and desserts.

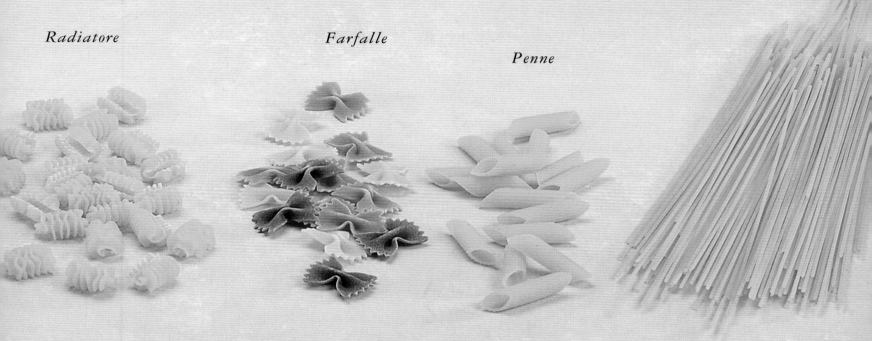

Radiatore

Farfalle

Penne

Spaghetti

Radiatore

Pasta comes in many different shapes, and this is one of the most interesting ones available. It looks like little curly radiators, hence the name. It is not as easily available as many of the more common pasta shapes. Children are keen on this one as it appeals to their sense of humour.

Farfalle

Farfalle is a delightful pasta which is made in different-sized bow shapes. It is attractive served with a colourful sauce and garnished. This pasta comes in several different colours which reflect their flavouring, including red (tomato), green (spinach) and white (egg).

Penne

This is a hollow, quill-like pasta, the ends of the tubes having been cut on the diagonal. It is a very versatile, popular pasta and can be bought either dried or fresh. Penne is boiled until it is just *al dente*, or firm to the bite, and served with any of the many classic pasta sauces.

Spaghetti

Spaghetti is probably the best known and most popular of all the pastas and can be bought either fresh or dried. It is also available in a low-fat form. There are a great many classic spaghetti dishes to choose from, two of the most famous ones being spaghetti bolognese and spaghetti carbonara.

Spaghetti
with Rocket & Ricotta

300 g/10 oz dried spaghetti
2 teaspoons olive oil
1 small onion, finely chopped
1 bunch of rocket, roots trimmed and leaves finely chopped
1 garlic clove, finely chopped
75 g/3 oz ricotta cheese
125 ml/4 fl oz dry white wine
salt and pepper

plunge the spaghetti into a large saucepan of salted boiling water and simmer for 10–12 minutes or until *al dente*.

meanwhile, heat the oil, then add the onion and cook gently, stirring for 5 minutes until softened.

add the rocket, garlic and salt and pepper to taste and stir for 2–3 minutes until the rocket is wilted. Add the ricotta and wine and stir until the ricotta has melted and is mixed evenly with the rocket.

drain the spaghetti, return to the pan and add the rocket mixture. Toss well to combine.

Serves 4
Preparation time: *10 minutes*
Cooking time: *12 minutes*

Kcal 330 • KJ 1396 • protein 12 g
• fat 5 g • CHO 59 g

clipboard: Rocket, also known as arugula, is a Mediterranean plant, which has a pungent, slightly peppery taste. The young leaves are particularly good in salads and pasta dishes. Spinach can be used instead of rocket, but in this case you will need to be generous with the pepper.

Tagliatelle Sicilienne

1 large aubergine, diced
1 tablespoon olive oil
2 onions, chopped
2 garlic cloves, chopped
1 x 400 g/13 oz can chopped plum tomatoes
2 teaspoons chopped basil
3.6 litres/6 pints water
375 g/12 oz fresh tagliatelle
salt and pepper

sprinkle the diced aubergine with salt and leave to drain for 30 minutes to remove any bitter taste. Rinse in cold water and dry well with kitchen paper.

heat the oil in a saucepan, add the onion, garlic and aubergines and cook for 2–3 minutes. Add the tomatoes and their juice, together with the basil, and season to taste. Simmer for 15–20 minutes.

meanwhile, bring the water to the boil in a large pan and add salt to taste. Put in the pasta, stir, and cook for 3–4 minutes until just *al dente*.

drain the pasta, turn it into a warm serving dish and top with the aubergine mixture. Serve sprinkled with reduced-fat grated Parmesan, if liked, but remember that this will add to the fat content.

Serves 4
Preparation time: *10 minutes, plus
  standing*
Cooking time: *15–20 minutes*

*Kcal 388 • KJ 1650 • protein 14 g
• fat 5 g • CHO 77 g*

Fettuccine
with Prawn Sauce

1 onion, chopped
2 garlic cloves, crushed
500 g/1 lb tomatoes, skinned and chopped
½ teaspoon dried basil
375 g/12 oz cooked peeled prawns
150 ml/¼ pint white wine
2 tablespoons chopped parsley
500 g/1 lb fettucine
salt and freshly ground black pepper

put the onion and garlic into a saucepan with a little water and simmer until soft.

add the tomatoes and basil, season with salt and pepper and simmer gently for 5 minutes. Stir in the prawns, wine and parsley and simmer for a further 10 minutes.

bring a large saucepan of salted water to the boil. Add the pasta, stir and cook for 10–12 minutes until *al dente*.

drain the pasta and place on a warm serving dish. Pour over the prawn sauce and serve at once.

Serves 4
Preparation time: *15 minutes*
Cooking time: *about 20 minutes*

kcal 579 • KJ 2460 • protein 37 g • fat 4 g • CHO 98 g

Dhal

This is an unusual lentil and tomato dish, which makes a particularly good accompaniment to many rice and meat dishes. Spicy flavours are added with ginger, chillies, coriander, cumin and garam masala.

250 g/8 oz dried green lentils, soaked in cold water overnight
1 medium onion, finely chopped
1 piece of fresh root ginger, bruised
2 bay leaves, crushed
2 fresh green chillies, chopped
1 tablespoon chopped fresh coriander
5 teaspoons olive oil
2 large garlic cloves, crushed
1 teaspoon ground coriander
½ teaspoon ground cumin
½ teaspoon garam masala
375 g/12 oz tomatoes, skinned, seeded and chopped
salt

drain the lentils and put them into a pan with the onion, root ginger, bay leaves, chillies, fresh coriander, 2 teaspoons of the oil, and sufficient water just to cover. Bring to the boil and simmer for about 45 minutes until the lentils are just tender. If the lentils become too dry, simply add a little extra liquid.

heat the remaining oil and fry the garlic for 4–5 minutes. Add the ground coriander, cumin, and garam masala and fry for 1 minute further. Add the tomatoes and salt to taste, and heat through.

stir the tomato and spice mixture into the lentils. Heat through gently for about 5 minutes.

serve piping hot.

Serves 4
Preparation time: *about 10 minutes*
Cooking time: *55 minutes*

kcal 225 • KJ 954 • protein 15 g • fat 5 g • CHO 32 g

clipboard: To bruise the ginger means to partially crush it with the heel of a knife or using a mortar and pestle. This releases its flavour. If you have a pressure cooker, use it to cook the lentils – they will take just 5 minutes. The addition of 75 g/3 oz cooked spinach gives the most wonderful texture to the dhal.

Couscous
with Hot Peppers

250 g/8 oz couscous
150 ml/¼ pint cold water
900 ml/1½ pints Vegetable Stock (see page 244)
2 celery sticks, chopped
2 large carrots, peeled and sliced
1 medium onion, peeled and thinly sliced
small bunch of herbs (one variety, or mixed)
2 garlic cloves, peeled and crushed
2 tablespoons raisins
25 g/1 oz chopped almonds
1 tablespoon chopped coriander
4 tomatoes, skinned, seeded and chopped
1 tablespoon chilli sauce
salt and freshly ground black pepper

put the couscous into a large mixing bowl; sprinkle half the cold water over evenly, and work in the couscous with your fingertips.

put the stock, vegetables, herbs and garlic into the base of the couscousier (see clipboard) and bring to the boil; put the moistened couscous into the top of the couscousier. Cover and steam over the stock for 30 minutes; stir the grains with your fingers once or twice during this time.

turn the couscous into a large bowl. Sprinkle with the remaining water and mix in with your fingers or a wooden spoon to separate the grains. Mix in the raisins, almonds, coriander, tomatoes, and salt and pepper to taste, and return the couscous to the top of the couscousier. Cover and steam for a further 30 minutes.

stir the chilli sauce into the stock in the base of the pan and heat through.

pile the hot couscous on to a warm serving dish and spoon the hot sauce and vegetables over the top. Serve immediately.

Serves 4
Preparation time: *about 30 minutes*
Cooking time: *1 hour*

*Kcal 234 • KJ 982 • protein 6 g
• fat 5 g • CHO 44 g*

clipboard: A special-purpose pan used for cooking couscous is called a couscousier. This is a type of double saucepan; the bottom pan usually contains the sauce and/or meat, and the top perforated pan contains the couscous grain, with a close-fitting lid on top. If you do not have such a pan, use a saucepan with a large sieve that will fit neatly over the top.

Meat

Spicy Lamb Kebabs

200 g/7 oz leg of lamb, cut into fine strips
4 small tomatoes, halved
125 g/4 oz button mushrooms
1 green pepper, cored, deseeded and cut
into 2.5 cm/1 inch squares
8 bay leaves (optional)

Marinade

150 ml/¼ pint low fat natural yogurt
juice of 1 lemon
2 teaspoons salt
1 teaspoon freshly ground black pepper
1 small onion, grated

trim all visible fat from the meat. Mix together all the marinade ingredients in a bowl. Place the meat in the marinade and leave for approximately 24 hours, turning occasionally.

reserve the marinade and thread the strips of meat on to 4 long or 8 short skewers, alternating with the tomatoes, mushrooms, pepper and the bay leaves, if using.

cook under a hot grill, turning once, for 10–15 minutes. Brush the vegetables with the marinade once or twice during cooking, to prevent them drying out. Serve with boiled rice and salad.

Serves 4
Preparation time: *30 minutes,*
  plus marinating
Cooking time: *10–15 minutes*

*Kcal 128 • KJ 540 • protein 14 g
• fat 5 g • CHO 7 g*

Lamb and Vegetable Hotpot

This is a comforting sort of dish, which is ideal for one of those cold wintry evenings when absolutely nothing else will do.

150 g/5 oz lean cooked lamb, cut into cubes
75 g/3 oz leeks, sliced
125 g/4 oz cauliflower, broken into florets
50 g/2 oz mushrooms, sliced
200 g/7 oz carrots, sliced
1 onion, sliced
2 tomatoes, sliced
150 ml/¼ pint Vegetable Stock (see page 244)
salt and freshly ground black pepper

remove any fat from the meat. Arrange the meat and vegetables, except the tomatoes, in layers in a casserole. Sprinkle on salt and pepper to taste, then arrange the tomato slices over the top. Pour in the vegetable stock and cover.

cook in the centre of a preheated moderate oven at 180°C/350°F/Gas Mark 4 for 45 minutes. Serve hot with broad beans, if liked.

Serves 3
Preparation time: *20 minutes*
Cooking time: *45 minutes*
Oven temperature:
  180°C/350°F/Gas Mark 4

Kcal 142 • KJ 597 • protein 18 g • fat 5 g • CHO 7 g

Thai Beef Salad

½ small Cos lettuce, shredded
1 stalk lemon grass, chopped very finely or
finely grated rind of ½ lemon
15 g/½ oz coriander leaves, torn into pieces
15 g/½ oz mint leaves, torn into pieces
1 small red onion, thinly sliced
1 garlic clove, crushed
2 green chillies, deseeded and chopped
1 tablespoon sesame oil
2 tablespoons lemon juice
1 tablespoon soft light brown sugar
375 g/12 oz lean, prime casserole steak, cut into
fine strips

arrange a bed of lettuce leaves on 6 individual plates. Mix together the lemon grass or lemon rind, coriander, mint and onion and scatter them over the lettuce. To make the dressing, combine the garlic, chillies, half the sesame oil, the lemon juice and sugar.

in a large frying pan or wok, heat the remaining oil and stir-fry the beef strips briskly for about 3 minutes, until lightly coloured. Toss the beef strips in the dressing, spoon it quickly over the salads and serve at once.

Serves 6
Preparation time: *20 minutes*
Cooking time: *3 minutes*

*Kcal 110 • KJ 464 • protein 13 g
• fat 5 g • CHO 3 g*

clipboard: Lemon grass is classified as a herb in its fresh state, but when it is dried – whether whole or in powdered form – it is regarded as a spice. It is an important flavouring in southeast Asian cuisine. When it is whole, the dried stalk should be soaked before it is used to flavour a dish, and then discarded before the dish is served. The powdered form is easier to use and does not need soaking. One teaspoon of powdered lemon grass is equivalent to one stalk of fresh lemon grass. It is more like lemon rind than lemon juice, and if you can't get hold of it you can use lemon peel instead.

Stir-Fried Beef
with Peppers

1 tablespoon olive oil
1 onion, finely sliced
1 large garlic clove, cut into thin strips
500 g/1 lb fillet steak, cut into thin strips
1 red pepper, cored, deseeded and cut into
matchstick strips
1 green pepper, cored, deseeded and cut into
matchstick strips
1 tablespoon soy sauce
2 tablespoons dry sherry
1 tablespoon chopped fresh rosemary
salt and pepper
rice, to serve (optional)

heat the olive oil in a wok or deep frying pan and stir-fry the onion and garlic for 2 minutes.

add the strips of beef and stir-fry briskly until evenly browned on all sides and almost tender.

add the strips of pepper and stir-fry for a further 2 minutes.

add the soy sauce, sherry, salt and pepper to taste and the rosemary, and stir-fry for a further 1–2 minutes. Serve hot with rice, if liked.

Serves 6
Preparation time: *5 minutes*
Cooking time: *10–12 minutes*

*Kcal 130 • KJ 550 • protein 16 g
• fat 5 g • CHO 3 g*

clipboard: Soy sauce is made from soya beans, wheat, water and salt. It has the same nutritional value as meat extract. It is routinely used in Chinese and Japanese cooking and may be used either in marinades or in the cooking process, or as a table condiment.

Italian Veal Casserole

Italian arborio rice, coloured with a little saffron, goes particularly well with this truly scrumptious dish.

15 g/½ oz low-fat spread
750 g/1½ lb pie veal, trimmed
seasoned flour, to dust
150 ml/¼ pint dry white wine
1 Spanish onion, finely chopped
750 g/1½ lb tomatoes, peeled and roughly chopped
1 teaspoon chopped lemon thyme
½ teaspoon dried oregano
150 ml/¼ pint Chicken Stock (see page 244)
1 lemon
2 cloves garlic, crushed (optional)
2 tablespoons chopped parsley
salt and freshly ground black pepper

heat the low-fat spread in a heavy-bottomed flameproof casserole. Cook the veal, lightly dusted with seasoned flour, until golden.

add the wine, onion, tomatoes, herbs, stock and seasoning. Bring to a simmering point, cover and cook gently for 1½–2 hours. Take off the lid after the first hour if the sauce needs reducing.

grate the rind of the lemon and mix with the garlic and parsley. Sprinkle over the casserole just before serving.

Serves 6
Preparation time: *30 minutes*
Cooking time: *1½–2 hours*

Kcal 177 • KJ 747 • protein 25 g • fat 5 g • CHO 5 g

Veal
with Apples and Calvados

Calvados adds a deliciously rich flavour to the sauce in this dish, but if you only have brandy to hand, you can use this instead.

6 veal chops or escalopes, weighing about
175 g/6 oz each
2 teaspoons soya or sunflower oil
I small onion, sliced finely
2 dessert apples, cored and sliced
25 g/I oz sultanas
125 ml/4 fl oz unsweetened apple juice
50 ml/2 fl oz Calvados
salt and freshly ground black pepper
parsley sprigs, to garnish

trim any visible fat from the veal chops or escalopes. Heat the oil in a flameproof casserole and fry the chops or escalopes for 3–4 minutes until they are lightly browned, turning them once. Add the onion and apple and fry lightly for a further 2 minutes. Stir in the sultanas, apple juice and Calvados. Season with salt and pepper.

cover the casserole with a lid. Place in a preheated oven at 190°C/375°F/Gas Mark 5 and bake for 50 minutes, or until the veal is tender. Remove the chops or escalopes from the casserole with a slotted spoon and place them on a warmed serving platter. Using the same spoon, arrange the apples, onions, and sultanas on top of the chops or escalopes. Garnish with parsley sprigs. Pour the cooking liquid over, or serve separately as a sauce.

Serves 6
Preparation time: *20 minutes*
Cooking time: *50 minutes*
Oven temperature: *190°C/375°F/Gas Mark 5*

Kcal 199 • KJ 839 • protein 29 g
• fat 5 g • CHO 9 g

Venison
Marinated in Beer

These venison cutlets are marinated in brown ale, which gives them a satisfyingly rich flavour. Serve hot with baked potatoes and a crisp salad.

4 lean venison cutlets
150 ml/¼ pint brown ale
3 teaspoons olive oil
1 garlic clove, crushed
2 dried bay leaves, crumbled
1 teaspoon soft light brown sugar
freshly ground black pepper

trim any visible fat from the venison cutlets and place them in a single layer in a shallow dish. Pour over the brown ale and olive oil.

add the garlic and bay leaves, pepper and sugar, but do not add salt. Cover the dish and place in the refrigerator to marinate for at least 4 hours, or overnight.

lift the venison out of the marinade, reserving the liquid. Place the cutlets on a hot barbecue and cook them for 10–12 minutes, turning once. They should be browned on the outside but slightly pink on the inside. Spoon over the marinade while cooking to prevent the meat drying out.

Serves 4
Preparation time: *20 minutes, plus marinating*
Cooking time: *10–12 minutes*

Kcal 216 • KJ 913 • protein 39 g • fat 5 g • CHO 2 g

Clipboard: This dish freezes particularly well. Freeze the venison in the marinade in a freezer proof container. This will keep for up to 1 month. Defrost in a refrigerator overnight.

Baked Jacket Potatoes
with Ham and Cheese

4 large baking potatoes, about 200 g/7 oz
each, scrubbed
250 g/8 oz cottage cheese
2 tablespoons chopped chives
150 g/5 oz lean cooked ham, trimmed of excess
fat and diced
chilli powder (optional)
freshly ground black pepper
2 tomatoes, quartered, to serve

prick the potatoes and wrap each one in a double thickness of foil. Place them in the coals at the edge of the barbecue, or in a preheated oven at 200°C/400°F/Gas Mark 6, and cook for about 45–60 minutes, turning them over occasionally.

while they are cooking, mix together the cheese, chives and ham, and seasoning. Open up the foil, cut a cross in the top of each potato and pinch the sides to open them. Spoon in the filling and sprinkle with a little chilli powder, if liked. Serve with the tomato quarters.

Serves 4
Preparation time: *15 minutes*
Cooking time: *45 minutes*
Oven temperature:
  200°C/400°F/Gas Mark 6

Kcal 257 • KJ 1086 • protein 20 g
• fat 5 g • CHO 36 g

clipboard: To microwave the potatoes, prick them and place in a ring on a double layer of kitchen paper. Cook on high power for 16–20 minutes, turning over once. Leave to stand for 5 minutes, then split and fill as above.

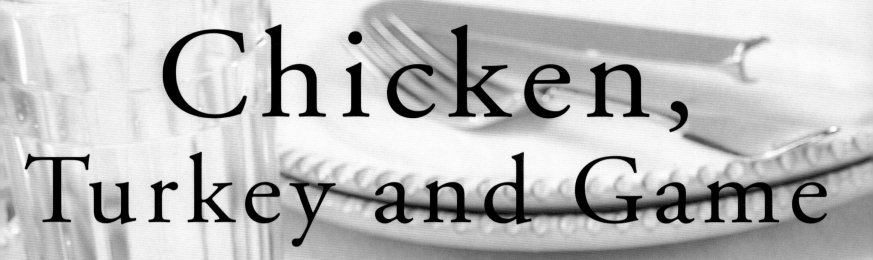

Chicken, Turkey and Game

Andalusian Chicken

1 x 1.75 kg/3½ lb roasting chicken
1 teaspoon dried mixed herbs
250 g/8 oz Spanish onions, chopped
500 g/1 lb green peppers, cored, deseeded and diced
4 tomatoes, peeled, seeded and roughly chopped
2 garlic cloves, crushed
1 teaspoon vegetable oil
250 g/8 oz peas, cooked
375 g/12 oz long-grain rice
pinch of saffron powder
bay leaf
salt and freshly ground black pepper

Garnish
lemon slices
chopped parsley

sprinkle the chicken with salt, pepper and herbs, and stand it in a roasting tin. Pour a cup of water round the chicken. Cover loosely with greased greaseproof paper or foil and roast in a moderately hot oven at 200°C/400°F/Gas Mark 6 for 1½ hours. Cool the chicken slightly, discard the skin, then strip the flesh from the bones and cut it into bite-sized pieces. Set aside. Use the chicken carcass and giblets to make chicken stock (see page 244), in which to cook the rice.

gently fry the onions, peppers, tomatoes and garlic in the oil until soft and golden. Stir in the cooked drained peas.

cook the rice in 900 ml/1½ pints chicken stock, with the saffron and bay leaf, for about 10 minutes, until tender. Drain if necessary (the rice should be quite dry) and remove the bay leaf.

now fold the chicken and rice into the onion and pepper mixture. Pile into a large, heated serving dish and garnish with the lemon slices. Serve sprinkled with parsley.

Serves 8
Preparation time: *30 minutes*
Cooking time: *1½ hours*
Oven temperature:
 200°C/400°F/Gas Mark 6

Kcal 312 • KJ 1320 • protein 24 g • fat 5 g • CHO 45 g

Lemon Chicken

1 tablespoon olive oil

1 small onion, finely sliced

4 chicken breasts, about 75 g/3 oz each, skinned and boned

2 tablespoons chopped fresh parsley

300 ml/½ pint Chicken Stock (see page 244)

1 tablespoon clear honey

juice of 1 lemon

2 teaspoons cornflour

1 tablespoon water

rind of 1 lemon, cut into matchstick strips

salt and pepper

heat the oil in a large frying pan. Add the onions and fry gently for 3–4 minutes. Add the chicken breasts and fry until lightly browned all over.

add the parsley, stock, honey, salt and pepper to taste and lemon juice. Cover the pan and simmer gently for 20 minutes.

using a slotted spoon, remove the chicken breasts to a warmed serving dish, and keep warm.

blend the cornflour and water to a smooth paste, stir in the hot cooking liquid, and then return to the pan. Stir over gentle heat until thickened. Add the strips of rind to the sauce and spoon evenly over the chicken.

Serves 4
Preparation time: *15 minutes*
Cooking time: *30–35 minutes*

Kcal 150 • KJ 630 • protein 17 g • fat 5 g • CHO 9 g

clipboard: Honey is more commonly known for its use in sweet dishes but it also has a place in many meat dishes such as this, and is a popular flavouring in savoury cooking round the world, including North Africa, China and the United States.

Stir-Fried Chicken
with Crunchy Vegetables

1 teaspoon vegetable oil
500 g/1 lb chicken breasts, skinned, boned and cut into thin strips across the grain
125 g/4 oz white cabbage, shredded finely
125 g/4 oz bean sprouts
1 large green pepper, cored, deseeded and cut lengthways into thin strips
2 medium carrots, cut lengthways into thin strips
2 cloves garlic, crushed
freshly ground black pepper

Sauce
2 teaspoons cornflour
4 tablespoons water
3 tablespoons soy sauce

prepare the sauce: mix the cornflour to a thin paste with the water, then stir in the soy sauce. Set aside.

heat the wok until hot. Add the oil and heat over a moderate heat. Add the chicken strips, increase the heat to high and stir-fry for 3–4 minutes or until lightly coloured on all sides.

remove the wok from the heat and transfer the chicken to a plate with a slotted spoon. Set aside.

return the wok to a moderate heat until hot. Add all the vegetables and the garlic and stir-fry for 2–3 minutes or until the green pepper is just beginning to soften.

stir the sauce to mix, then pour into the wok. Increase the heat to high and toss the ingredients until the sauce thickens and coats the vegetables. Add the chicken with its juices and toss for 1–2 minutes or until all the ingredients are combined. Add pepper to taste and serve at once.

Serves 4 as a main dish
Preparation time: *15 minutes*
Cooking time: *6–10 minutes*

Kcal 197 • KJ 830 • protein 30 g
• fat 5 g • CHO 8 g

Spiced Chicken

1 teaspoon coarsely ground cinnamon
6 chicken drumsticks, skinned
2 boned and skinned chicken breasts, about
125 g/4 oz each, cut into cubes
300 ml/½ pint natural yogurt
2 large onions, chopped
2 fresh green chillies, deseeded and chopped
1 teaspoon cumin seed
1 garlic clove, peeled and chopped
1 tablespoon sweet paprika
2 tablespoons Chicken Stock (see page 244)
½ teaspoon finely grated lemon rind
1 red pepper, cored, deseeded and chopped
1 tablespoon cornflour
salt and freshly ground black pepper

rub the cinnamon into the chicken meat, combine with the yogurt and marinate for about 30 minutes.

lightly fry the onions, chillies, cumin and garlic in a casserole. Stir in the paprika.

strain the chicken meat, reserving the yogurt.

add the chicken to the casserole, stir well to coat and then add the stock, lemon rind, red pepper and half of the reserved yogurt. Cover and simmer slowly for about 1 hour.

combine the cornflour with the remaining yogurt and stir it into the casserole a few minutes before serving, then bring to the boil and simmer for 1–2 minutes. Season to taste.

serve with rice.

Serves 6
Preparation time: *10 minutes, plus
30 minutes marinating time*
Cooking time: *about 1¼ hours*

*Kcal 186 • KJ 784 • protein 23 g
• fat 5 g • CHO 13 g*

clipboard: Chicken absorbs the flavours of spices very well, as here. Cinnamon, chillies and sweet paprika are used in this recipe to produce an excellent combination of tastes.

Chicken and Courgette Bake

This is a simple supper dish, which is particularly good served with a fresh green salad.

750 g/1½ lb courgettes, sliced diagonally
50 g/2 oz reduced-fat Edam cheese, grated
175 g/6 oz cooked chicken, skinned and diced
75 g/3 oz cooked ham, diced
3 tomatoes, sliced

Sauce
25 g/1 oz low-fat spread
25 g/1 oz plain flour
300 ml/½ pint skimmed milk
1 tablespoon sherry (optional)
salt and freshly ground black pepper

preheat the oven to 190°C/375°F/Gas Mark 5.

cook the courgettes in boiling salted water for 4–5 minutes. Drain well on kitchen paper towels and place in an ovenproof dish.

sprinkle with 25 g/1 oz of the cheese. Arrange the chicken, ham and tomatoes in layers over the top and sprinkle with the remaining cheese.

make the sauce: melt the low-fat spread in a small saucepan over a moderate heat. Stir in the flour and cook for 1 minute. Gradually add the milk, stirring continuously. Bring the sauce to the boil and let it cook for 2–3 minutes. Season to taste and blend in the sherry, if using. Pour the sauce over the meat, courgettes and tomatoes. Bake in the oven for 20 minutes until golden. Serve hot.

Serves 6
Preparation time: *15 minutes*
Cooking time: *20 minutes*
Oven temperature:
  190°C/375°F/Gas Mark 5

Kcal 157 • KJ 660 • protein 18 g
• fat 5 g • CHO 9 g

Chicken with Ginger

375 g/12 oz boneless chicken breasts, skinned
1 tablespoon dry sherry
4 spring onions, chopped
1 x 2.5 cm/1 inch piece fresh root ginger,
finely chopped
3 teaspoons oil
1–2 garlic cloves, thinly sliced
2 celery sticks, sliced diagonally
1 small green pepper, cored, deseeded and sliced
2 tablespoons light soy sauce
juice of ½ lemon
shredded rind of 2 lemons
¼ teaspoon chilli powder

Garnish
lemon wedges
parsley sprigs

cut the chicken into 7.5 cm/3 inch strips. Combine the sherry, spring onions and ginger, add the chicken and toss well to coat, then set aside to marinate for 15 minutes.

heat the oil in a large non-stick frying pan or wok. Add the garlic, celery and green pepper and stir-fry for 1 minute. Add the chicken and marinade and cook for 2 minutes. Stir in the soy sauce, lemon juice and rind and chilli powder and cook for a further 1 minute.

pile into a warmed serving dish, garnish with lemon wedges and parsley sprigs and serve immediately.

Serves 4
Preparation time: *20 minutes, plus marinating*
Cooking time: *4–5 minutes*

Kcal 142 • KJ 598 • protein 21 g • fat 5 g • CHO 2 g

clipboard: If you cannot find any fresh root ginger locally, use the dried kind. The best quality ginger comes from Jamaica and is usually available in markets supplying ethnic communities as well as in some large supermarkets.

Chicken en Cocotte

1 x 1.5 kg/3 lb chicken, jointed and skinned
1 teaspoon vegetable oil
25 g/1 oz lean smoked ham, diced
4 small onions, chopped
1 clove garlic, crushed
2 tablespoons brandy
6 tomatoes, peeled and chopped
3 carrots, chopped
2 sticks celery, cut into 4 cm/1½ inch lengths
¼ teaspoon chopped thyme
bay leaf
300 ml/½ pint red wine
salt and freshly ground black pepper
chopped parsley, to garnish

season the chicken portions with salt and pepper. Heat the oil in a flameproof casserole or flambé pan and add the diced ham and chicken portions. Cook until golden, turning. Take out the meats and set aside.

fry the onions and garlic in the pan fat until softened, stirring. Return the chicken and ham to the pan. Pour on the brandy and flambé the meat. Now add the tomatoes, carrots, celery, thyme, bay leaf and red wine. Bring to the boil, cover and simmer for about 30 minutes, until the chicken and vegetables are tender. Remove the bay leaf before serving and sprinkle with chopped parsley.

Serves 6
Preparation time: *30 minutes*
Cooking time: *30 minutes*

Kcal 188 • KJ 789 • protein 23 g • fat 5 g • CHO 2 g

clipboard: Bay leaves are not true herbs, as the bay tree grows up to 18 m/60 feet high but, being so highly aromatic, they have always been treated as such. They are an important ingredient in the bouquet garni and are commonly used to flavour fish and meat stocks, court-bouillons and soups, pâtés and casseroles. They may be used either fresh off the tree or dried, and require long, slow cooking in order to make the most of their flavour.

Chicken
with Mango Sauce

Chicken and mango is a truly delicious combination. Fresh peaches may be used instead.

1 large ripe mango
200 ml/7 fl oz Chicken Stock (see page 244)
3 tablespoons dry white wine
juice of ½ lemon
400 g/13 oz chicken breasts, skinned and boned
15 g/½ oz low-fat spread
1 teaspoon pink peppercorns
2 tablespoons low-fat natural yogurt or
Homemade Yogurt (see page 247)
salt and freshly ground black pepper

halve the mango and remove the stone. Cut 8 thin slices from the better-looking half of the mango. Scoop all the flesh from the remaining mango.

put the mango flesh into a liquidiser or food processor with the chicken stock, white wine and lemon juice, and blend until smooth.

fry the chicken breasts in the low-fat spread until evenly browned on all sides. Season, add the mango sauce and simmer, covered, for about 8 minutes.

stir in the pink peppercorns and the yogurt, and heat through. Arrange on a warm serving dish and garnish with the slices of mango.

Serves 4
Preparation time: *25 minutes*
Cooking time: *about 15 minutes*

*Kcal 180 • KJ 757 • protein 24 g
• fat 5 g • CHO 8 g*

clipboard: The mango stone runs lengthways through the fruit. To remove it, insert the tip of a small knife at one or two points to find out which way it is running. Insert a sharp knife at one end of the mango and cut through, keeping the blade of the knife as close to the stone as possible. Repeat with the other half of the mango.

Stuffed Pot-Roasted Chicken

125 g/4 oz long-grain rice
1 x 1.5 kg/3 lb chicken, with giblets
Chicken Stock (see page 244)
50 g/2 oz raisins
1 small green pepper, cored, deseeded and chopped
grated rind of 1 lemon
500 g/1 lb onions, quartered
500 g/1 lb baby carrots
500 g/1 lb small tomatoes, peeled and quartered
¼ teaspoon chopped rosemary
300 ml/½ pint dry cider
lemon juice
salt and freshly ground black pepper
chopped parsley, to garnish

cook the rice in boiling salted water for 10 minutes, until tender. Drain well. Chop the chicken liver roughly and cook for a few minutes in a little stock. Drain. Mix together the rice, chicken livers, raisins, green pepper, grated lemon rind and seasoning. Stuff the chicken with this mixture.

grease a casserole dish large enough to hold the chicken comfortably. Place the onions, carrots and tomatoes in the bottom and lay the chicken on top. Sprinkle the chicken with the rosemary and pour over the cider.

cover the casserole and cook in a moderate oven at 180°C/350°F/Gas Mark 4 for 2 hours, until the chicken is tender. Remove the lid for the last 10 minutes to brown the chicken.

lift out the chicken and place on a hot serving dish. Remove the vegetables carefully with a slotted spoon and arrange round the chicken. Strain the juices from the casserole into a small pan and add a squeeze of lemon juice. Reheat and serve separately, in a jug or sauceboat. Serve the chicken with boiled potatoes tossed in the chopped parsley.

Serves 6
Preparation time: *30 minutes*
Cooking time: *2 hours 10 minutes*
Oven temperature:
180°C/350°F/Gas Mark 4

Kcal 299 • KJ 1258 • protein 25 g • fat 5 g • CHO 35 g

Roast Chicken with Tarragon

This great way of roasting a chicken part steams and part roasts, which preserves the juices and the flavour.

1 x 1.5 kg/3 lb roasting chicken, with giblets
chopped tarragon, fresh or dried
twist of lemon peel
cornflour to thicken
white wine or lemon juice
salt and freshly ground black pepper
sprigs of fresh tarragon, to garnish

remove the giblets from the chicken. Sprinkle the inside of the chicken with salt, pepper and a little tarragon, then place the twist of lemon peel inside. Scatter some more tarragon over the outside. Season lightly. Place the chicken in a roasting tin with the giblets and pour in 300 ml/½ pint of hot water. Cover the tin loosely with foil and cook in a moderately hot oven at 200°C/400°F/Gas Mark 6 for about 1¼ hours. Check occasionally during cooking that the liquid in the tin has not dried out, and add a little more water if it looks low.

when the chicken is ready, the leg joint should move freely and when the leg meat is pierced with a fine skewer, the juice that runs should be clear. Lift the chicken on to a hot carving dish and remove the giblets. Pour off any fat from the juices left in the pan and thicken with a little cornflour moistened in cold water. Add a dash of white wine or a squeeze of lemon juice and strain. Garnish with the tarragon and serve with seasoned vegetables. Do not eat the chicken skin.

Serves 6
Preparation time: *20 minutes*
Cooking time: *1 hour 15 minutes*
Oven temperature: *200°C/400°F/Gas Mark 6*

Kcal 150 • KJ 629 • protein 24 g
• fat 5 g • CHO 1 g

Grilled Devilled Chicken

Mustard, ginger, Worcestershire sauce, sugar and lemon are used in this traditional recipe to give the chicken a bit of a kick! Serve with a green salad and rice pilaf.

625 g/1¼ lb chicken portions, skinned
1 tablespoon French mustard
1 teaspoon ground ginger
1 teaspoon salt
1 teaspoon freshly ground black pepper
1 teaspoon Worcestershire sauce
½ teaspoon sugar
juice of 1 lemon

place the chicken portions in a shallow ovenproof dish. Mix together the mustard, ginger, salt, pepper, Worcestershire sauce, sugar and lemon juice. Use to coat the chicken portions and leave to marinate for several hours, turning occasionally in the marinade.

place the chicken portions under a preheated grill or on a barbecue, not too close to the coals. Allow 15–20 minutes on each side, although the cooking time may be shorter if you do this on an outside barbecue.

Serves 4
Preparation time: *10 minutes, plus marinating*
Cooking time: *30–40 minutes*

kcal 187 • KJ 787 • protein 33 g • fat 5 g • CHO 2 g

Traditional Roast Turkey

1 x 5 kg/10 lb turkey
1 tablespoon dried basil
600 ml/1 pint Chicken or Vegetable Stock (see page 244)
5 tablespoons port
1 tablespoon cornflour
salt and freshly ground black pepper

Stuffings
500 g/1 lb chestnuts
175 g/6 oz mashed potato
65 g/2½ oz fresh breadcrumbs
1 heaped tablespoon sultanas
1 garlic clove, crushed
2 celery sticks, finely chopped
2 tablespoons chopped parsley
grated rind of 1 lemon
a little grated fresh root ginger
3 tablespoons medium-dry sherry
salt and freshly ground black pepper

prepare the stuffings for the neck and carcass in advance. Make a slit on the rounded side of the chestnuts. Drop, four at a time, into a small pan of boiling water for 3 minutes. Peel and skin. Cook the chestnuts gently in fresh boiling water for about 20 minutes. Drain, then mash with a fork. Mix a quarter of the chestnuts with the mashed potato and salt and pepper. Use to stuff the neck of the bird. Mix the remaining chestnuts with the rest of the stuffing ingredients and use to stuff the turkey carcass.

stand the bird in a large roasting tin and sprinkle with basil and salt and pepper. Pour the stock round the bird and cover the tin loosely with a piece of greased foil. Cook in a moderate oven at 180°C/350°F/Gas Mark 4, allowing 15–20 minutes per 500 g/1 lb, plus 20 minutes extra. Turn the turkey, on its side or upright, every 30 minutes, and baste frequently.

remove the foil 20 minutes before the end of the cooking time, to brown the bird, turning it breast side up. Pour off the pan juices to make gravy. Skim off all the fat and boil up the juices with the port. Moisten the cornflour with a little cold water and stir into the gravy, to thicken. Keep warm in a sauceboat until ready to serve. Remember not to eat the turkey skin, which is the most fatty part of the bird. Serve with vegetables.

Serves 8–10
Preparation time: *45 minutes*
Cooking time: *3 hours 10 minutes–4 hours*
Oven temperature: *180°C/350°F/Gas Mark 4*

per serving of 100 g/3½ oz of meat: kcal 290
• KJ 1223 • protein 31 g • fat 5 g • CHO 29 g

Turkey in Vermouth

White vermouth gives an unusual and interesting flavour to this turkey recipe. The stuffing, which contains lemon rind, herbs, breadcrumbs and grapes, is another successful addition.

1 x 3.5–4 kg/7–8 lb turkey
1 tablespoon chopped tarragon
1 small onion, chopped
2 sticks celery, chopped
4 medium-sized carrots, chopped
300 ml/½ pint dry white vermouth

Stuffing
75 g/3 oz fresh white breadcrumbs
grated rind of 1½ lemons
4 tablespoons chopped parsley
½ tablespoon chopped thyme
125 g/4 oz green grapes, halved and pipped
1 egg, beaten
salt and freshly ground black pepper

mix together the dry stuffing ingredients and bind with a little egg. Do not make the mixture too wet. Spoon the stuffing into the bird. Sprinkle the turkey with the chopped tarragon. Lay the onion, celery and carrots in the base of a large oblong casserole dish or roasting tin. Place the turkey on the bed of vegetables and pour round the vermouth. Cover and cook in a moderately hot oven at 190°C/375°F/Gas Mark 5 for 2½–3 hours, or until cooked. Baste from time to time with the pan juices. Add a little hot giblet stock or water, if necessary, to keep the dish moist.

slice the turkey, which should be succulent and tender, and serve with a spoonful of stuffing and the strained juices from the casserole. Remember not to eat the turkey skin.

Serves 6
Preparation time: *20 minutes*
Cooking time: *2½–3 hours*
Oven temperature: *190°C/375°F/Gas Mark 5*

Kcal 265 • KJ 1118 • protein 31 g • fat 4 g • CHO 15 g

Turkey Burgers

with Barbecue Sauce

Serve these burgers with wholemeal baps and a varied selection of relishes and salads.

1 kg/2 lb turkey meat, minced
1 onion, finely chopped
1 tablespoon white wine
1 teaspoon chopped fresh tarragon or parsley
salt and pepper

Sauce

15 g/½ oz low-fat spread
1 medium onion, finely sliced
2 garlic cloves, crushed
1 green pepper, cored, deseeded and sliced
125 g/4 oz mushrooms, sliced
1 x 400 g/13 oz can chopped tomatoes
2 teaspoons dried oregano
1 teaspoon Tabasco sauce
salt and pepper

place the minced turkey in a large bowl and add the onion, wine and herbs. Mix together well and season to taste. Shape into 12 burgers. Place on a baking tray and set aside.

to make the sauce, melt the low-fat spread in a pan over a moderate heat. Cook the onion and garlic until pale golden. Add the pepper and continue cooking for 5 minutes. Add the mushrooms, tomatoes and oregano and cook for a further 5–10 minutes. Add the Tabasco and season to taste.

heat the grill to moderate and grill the burgers, brushing with a little sunflower oil if necessary, for about 7 minutes on each side until cooked.

serve immediately, with the sauce served separately.

Serves 6
Preparation time: *30 minutes*
Cooking time: *20–25 minutes*

Kcal 382 • KJ 1613 • protein 79 g • fat 5 g • CHO 5 g

clipboard: Chicken may be used in place of turkey. The burgers can be cooked on a barbecue instead of under the grill.

Sweet and Sour Chinese Turkey

500 g/1 lb turkey breast
2 tablespoons lemon juice
5 tablespoons orange juice
4–5 celery sticks
2 sharon fruit or firm tomatoes
8–10 radishes
½ Chinese cabbage
1 large green pepper, cored and deseeded
1 tablespoon oil
150 ml/¼ pint Chicken Stock (see page 244)
1½ teaspoons cornflour
1 tablespoon soy sauce
1 tablespoon clear honey

cut the turkey breast into thin strips. Marinate in the lemon and orange juice for 30 minutes.

cut the celery, sharon fruit or tomatoes, radishes, Chinese cabbage and green pepper into small neat pieces. Heat the oil in a large non-stick frying pan or wok.

drain the turkey and reserve the marinade. Fry the turkey in the oil until nearly tender. Add the vegetables and sharon fruit or tomatoes and heat for 2–3 minutes only. Blend the chicken stock with the marinade and the cornflour. Add the soy sauce and honey. Pour this mixture over the ingredients in the pan and stir until thickened. Serve immediately.

Serves 4
Preparation time: *15 minutes, plus marinating*
Cooking time: *15–20 minutes*

Kcal 198 • KJ 835 • protein 29 g • fat 5 g • CHO 11 g

clipboard: Sharon fruit is a variety of persimmon which can be eaten like an apple. The skin is edible or the fruit can be peeled, as you prefer. It is often candied.

Turkey and Parma Ham Kebabs

500 g/1 lb turkey fillet, cut into 4 cm/1½ inch cubes
grated rind of 1 lemon
1 small onion, finely chopped
1 garlic clove, finely chopped
1 teaspoon pesto sauce
2 teaspoons oil
125 g/4 oz Parma ham, cut into long strips
8 small button mushrooms
8 small bay leaves
8 wedges of lemon
salt and freshly ground pepper
shredded lettuce, to serve

put the turkey into a shallow dish. Mix the lemon rind with the onion, garlic, pesto and oil and season to taste.

stir the marinade into the turkey, cover and chill for 3–4 hours.

drain the turkey, reserving the marinade. Wrap each piece of turkey in a strip of Parma ham.

thread the turkey and ham rolls on to kebab skewers, alternating with the mushrooms, bay leaves and wedges of lemon.

brush the threaded skewers with the marinade, grill for 4–5 minutes. Turn the kebab skewers, brush once again with the marinade, and grill for a further 4–5 minutes.

serve piping hot on a bed of shredded lettuce.

Serves 4
Preparation time: *20 minutes, plus marinating*
Cooking time: *10 minutes*

Kcal 180 • KJ 756 • protein 32 g • fat 5 g • CHO 2 g

clipboard: The ham will wrap round the turkey more easily if it is moist. It is important, therefore, to keep it closely covered in the refrigerator so that it does not dry out.

Rabbit with Rosemary *and Mustard*

1 medium onion, finely chopped
1 teaspoon olive oil
4 rabbit joints, about 200 g/7 oz each
300 ml/½ pint Chicken Stock (see page 244)
200 ml/7 fl oz dry white wine
2 teaspoons coarse-grain mustard
1 tablespoon chopped rosemary
3 tablespoons low-fat fromage frais
1 egg yolk
salt and freshly ground black pepper
sprigs of fresh rosemary, to garnish

fry the onion gently in the olive oil for 3 minutes. Add the rabbit joints and brown evenly on all sides.

add the chicken stock, white wine, mustard, rosemary, and salt and pepper to taste. Cover and simmer for 45 minutes until the rabbit is just tender.

remove the rabbit joints to a serving dish and keep warm.

boil the cooking liquid rapidly until reduced by half; beat the fromage frais with the egg yolk and whisk into the cooking liquid over a gentle heat, without boiling.

spoon the sauce over the rabbit and garnish with sprigs of rosemary.

Serves 4
Preparation time: *about 10 minutes*
Cooking time: *about 55 minutes*

Kcal 172 • KJ 719 • protein 18 g • fat 5 g • CHO 5 g

clipboard: If you are using frozen rabbit, make sure the joints are completely thawed before cooking. Other mustards can be used but they will not give quite the same pungency and texture as coarse-grain mustard.

Desserts

Marinated Nectarines

4 large ripe nectarines
I lemon
I large orange
200 ml/7 fl oz water
4 tablespoons dry vermouth

skin the nectarines. Peel the lemon thinly and cut into matchstick strips. Squeeze the lemon juice into a large bowl and fill up with iced water. Put the prepared nectarines into the lemon water.

peel the orange thinly, removing all the pith; chop the flesh into pieces, discarding any pips. Cut the orange peel into matchstick strips. Put the orange flesh into a liquidizer or blender with the water and vermouth, and blend until smooth.

lift the nectarines out of the lemon water and drain. Put the nectarines into a shallow dish and spoon over the prepared orange and vermouth sauce. Cover and chill for 2 hours – no longer or the nectarines are likely to discolour.

sprinkle with the strips of lemon and orange peel and serve immediately.

Serves 4
Preparation time: *25 minutes, plus chilling*

Kcal 88 • KJ 377 • protein 2 g • fat 0 g • CHO 17 g

clipboard: To skin a nectarine, nick the stalk end with a sharp knife and plunge the fruit into boiling water for 45 seconds. The skin will then slide off easily.

Seasonal Berries

250 g/8 oz blackcurrants, topped and tailed
500 g/1 lb strawberries, hulled and quartered or
halved, according to size
500 g/1 lb raspberries, hulled
250 g/8 oz cultivated blackberries, topped and tailed
250 g/8 oz loganberries, hulled
300 ml/½ pint rosé wine
½ teaspoon ground allspice

combine all the berries in a serving bowl.

heat the wine in a saucepan to boiling point, add the allspice and pour over the fruit at once.

cool and stand at room temperature for 4–6 hours before serving.

Serves 4
Preparation time: *10 minutes*
Cooking time: *5 minutes, plus standing*

kcal 156 • KJ 658 • protein 4 g • fat 1 g • CHO 23 g

clipboard: Allspice is the berry of an evergreen tree that grows wild in South America and the West Indies. It is also known as Jamaican pepper. The flavour is reminiscent of a mixture of other spices, including cinnamon, cloves and nutmeg. An easy substitute for allspice is to mix equal quantities of ground cinnamon and mace with a half part each of ground cloves and ground pepper. It can be used in both sweet and savoury dishes.

Citrus Fruit Salad

2 limes, peeled and thinly sliced
1 small lemon, peeled and segmented
4 sweet oranges, peeled and coarsely chopped
4 mandarins, peeled and coarsely chopped
2–3 grapefruit, peeled and coarsely chopped
1 teaspoon granulated sugar
1 teaspoon Angostura bitters
3 tablespoons sparkling mineral water
12 kumquats (optional)
1 bunch fresh mint
shredded mint leaves, to garnish

using a potato peeler, take a wafer-thin sliver from the discarded skins of all the citrus fruit except the kumquats.

using a pestle and mortar, crush the slivers with the sugar to release the highly flavoured oils, combine with the Angostura bitters and mineral water and set aside.

place the fruit in a deep bowl. Halve the unpeeled kumquats and add them. Strain the mineral water and stir it in.

plunge the bunch of fresh mint, tied with a piece of thread, in and out of boiling water, then straight into the fruit. Chill, covered, for 2 hours.

remove the mint before serving and stir in the shredded mint leaves.

Serves 6
Preparation time: *45–55 minutes, plus chilling*

Kcal 126 • KJ 533 • protein 3 g • fat 0 g • CHO 29 g

clipboard: The mixture of all these different citrus fruits – lime, lemon, orange, mandarin and grapefruit is wonderful. If the fruit salad is too sharp, add 1 tablespoon honey, which you have heated slightly beforehand so that it mixes in easily.

Pears with Fresh Raspberry Sauce

The combination of pears with fresh, mouth-puckering raspberry sauce is magic.

4 large firm pears
300 ml/½ pint orange juice
bay leaf
small piece of cinnamon stick
1 tablespoon clear honey
250 g/8 oz fresh raspberries

peel and halve the pears, then core them. Place them in a saucepan with the orange juice, bay leaf, cinnamon stick and honey. Cover the pan and simmer gently for 10 minutes.

turn the pear halves over in their cooking liquid; cover the pan and leave them to cool in their liquid.

blend the raspberries in a liquidizer until smooth. Add enough pear cooking liquid to give a thin coating consistency.

arrange the drained pear halves in a shallow serving dish and trickle over the prepared sauce.

Serves 4
Preparation time: *about 20 minutes, plus cooling*
Cooking time: *10 minutes*

Kcal 126 • KJ 516 • protein 7 g • fat 2 g • CHO 31 g

clipboard: Another way of serving these pears is to spoon the raspberry sauce on to individual serving plates. Trickle a little plain unsweetened yogurt on top, and arrange the pear halves carefully on top.

Wholemeal Fruit Pancakes

Pancakes
50 g/2 oz plain wholemeal flour
50 g/2 oz plain flour, sifted
1 egg, beaten
300 ml/½ pint skimmed milk
sunflower oil, for frying

Filling
3 large oranges, peeled, segmented and chopped
475 g/15 oz can pineapple pieces in natural juice
25 g/1 oz walnuts, chopped
2 teaspoons arrowroot
150 ml/¼ pint pure orange juice
2 tablespoons Kirsch (optional)

make the pancake batter: place the flours in a mixing bowl and make a well in the centre. Add the egg and mix in well with a wooden spoon. Pour in half the milk slowly and beat thoroughly. Add the remaining milk and stir well so that the batter has a smooth, creamy consistency.

heat a little oil in a 15 cm/6 inch non-stick frying pan. Pour a little batter into the pan. Tilt the pan to spread the batter thinly and evenly. Cook until golden brown, then turn over and cook the other side. Repeat until all the batter has been used. Stack the pancakes on a warmed plate with rounds of greaseproof paper between them. Keep warm.

prepare the filling: place the orange pieces in a bowl. Drain the pineapple and reserve the juice. Chop the pineapple and add it to the orange with the walnuts. Blend the arrowroot with a little of the pineapple juice until smooth. Place the arrowroot mixture, pineapple and orange juice in a small pan. Bring to the boil over a moderate heat, stirring continuously until smooth and thickened. Add Kirsch, if using.

pour a little sauce over the fruit and nuts to coat them. Mix together. Spoon the filling down the centre of the pancakes and fold into triangles. Transfer to a warmed serving dish and serve. Serve the sauce separately.

Serves 6
Preparation time: *30 minutes*
Cooking time: *30 minutes*

Kcal 200 • KJ 850 • protein 7 g
• fat 5 g • CHO 35 g

Honeyed Apples

Nuts, dates, lemon, honey and cinnamon – this combination is true bliss!

4 medium-sized cooking apples, cored
1 tablespoon chopped nuts, toasted
1 tablespoon chopped dates
juice of ½ lemon
about 2 tablespoons clear honey
½ teaspoon ground cinnamon

wash the apples and peel the top half. Place in an ovenproof dish. Mix the remaining ingredients together and use to fill the centres of the apples.

pour a little more honey over the apples and cook, covered, in a moderately hot oven at 190°C/375°F/Gas Mark 5 for about 45 minutes.

Serves 4
Preparation time: *20 minutes*
Cooking time: *45 minutes*
Oven temperature: *190°C/375°F/Gas Mark 5*

Kcal 123 • KJ 526 • protein 2 g • fat 2 g • CHO 27 g

Fruit

Apples

Peaches

Strawberries

Dried figs

Dried dates

Dried figs

Fig trees grow in the Mediterranean region, including Greece, Italy and the south of France, Asia Minor and North Africa. A fragile fruit, it does not travel particularly well and is therefore often dried or preserved. It makes delicious jams and various puddings, as well as being a pleasing addition to salads. It goes well with prosciutto.

Dried dates

The date comes originally from Turkey. It is a highly nutritious fruit, being an excellent source of both vitamins and minerals. It can be used in many delicious sweet and savoury dishes, and goes particularly well with walnuts – hence the successful pairing of these two ingredients in many date and walnut breads and cakes.

Strawberries

The history of the strawberry is said to go back to Roman times and remains today one of our most highly prized summer fruits. A juicy red berry with seed-pitted skin, it is best eaten simply – either on its own straight from the stalk or with the addition of cream – and requires remarkably little to be done to it in the kitchen.

Peaches

Said to be the emblem of immortality, the peach is a Chinese fruit which came to Europe with the Romans. With its velvet downy skin and its succulent white or yellow flesh, it is the perfect dessert fruit, or it can be incorporated into fruit salads or used to make a variety of delicious tarts and compôtes. It also makes a tasty fruit juice.

Apples

The apple probably originated in southwest Asia but hundreds of varieties are now grown widely all over the world. There are thousands of classified varieties, which may be green, red or yellow with a creamy white flesh. They are usually eaten raw, but can also be stewed, baked, or used in a variety of desserts including tarts and pies.

Mangoes

Limes

Apricots

Redcurrants

Mangoes

The mango originated in India, and Buddha himself is said to have reposed in a mango grove. A perfectly ripe mango, with its smooth skin and its sweet green, yellow, orange or pink flesh, requires no further improvement. It is the perfect addition to fruit salads, it makes a truly delicious ice cream, and no curry is complete without the addition of a spoonful or two of mango, or mango and lime, chutney.

Limes

The lime tree is the smallest member of the citrus family of trees, and has the smallest fruits. But don't be fooled by its size: lime juice is aromatic, sharp and refreshing, and carries an even bigger punch than lemon juice.

Apricots

Providing that it is at just the right state of ripeness and in absolutely perfect condition, the apricot is one of the most delectable fruits that you can eat. It is in season in the late summer. Said to have been brought to Europe from northern China in the 16th century, the apricot became popular in Middle Eastern Cookery, largely because of its perfect compatibility with lamb. It is delicious either raw or cooked, and is suitable in both sweet and savoury dishes. It can be made into wine, and is also available dried. Given its tremendous versatility, the apricot deserves a special place in every cook's repertoire.

Redcurrants

Redcurrants can be eaten fresh, although fresh redcurrants can sometimes be a little on the tart side for some people's tastes. The sharpness of the redcurrant makes it the perfect accompaniment to certain meats, particularly game and turkey, in the form of the best-known fruit jelly in the world. Redcurrants are especially good, too, when they are made into fruit tarts and summer puddings.

Sliced Figs with Lemon Sauce

8 plump ripe fresh figs
2 tablespoons lemon juice
150 ml/¼ pint unsweetened apple purée
grated rind of ½ lemon
3 tablespoons plain unsweetened yogurt
artificial sweetener
1 tablespoon chopped pistachio nuts
4 twists of lemon peel, to decorate (optional)

cut each fig into 4 wedges. (Alternatively, the figs can be sliced, provided they are not too soft.) Sprinkle the cut figs with lemon juice.

mix the apple purée with the lemon rind and yogurt. Add sweetener to taste and half the chopped pistachios.

spoon a pool of the lemon and pistachio sauce on to each of 4 small plates and arrange the pieces of fig decoratively on top.

sprinkle with the remaining pistachio nuts and decorate with twists of lemon peel, if liked.

Serves 4
Preparation time: *15–20 minutes*

Kcal 124 • KJ 524 • protein 5 g • fat 4 g • CHO 18 g

clipboard: Figs have a very short season, so look out for them in the shops and grab them as soon as you can. The recipe for this dish was made in heaven!

Chocolate Soufflé

vegetable oil, for greasing
75 ml/3 fl oz fresh orange juice
75 g/3 oz sugar
4 large egg whites
25 g/I oz unsweetened cocoa powder
2 tablespoons orange liqueur
125 g/4 oz low-fat vanilla ice cream, softened
fine strips of orange zest or sprigs of
mint, to decorate

grease 6 cups with the oil.

heat the orange juice and sugar in a small saucepan for 3–4 minutes over medium to high heat, stirring occasionally, until the mixture takes on a syrupy consistency. Remove from the heat.

beat the egg whites in a large bowl until stiff, stopping before dry peaks form. Pour the syrup over the egg whites and beat for 2 minutes. Add the cocoa powder and liqueur and beat only until well mixed. Pour into the prepared cups.

bake in a preheated oven at 150°C/300°F/Gas Mark 2 for 10–12 minutes or until the soufflés are puffed. Be careful not to overbake the soufflés or they will become tough. Cooking time will vary slightly depending on size of cups used.

spoon 2 tablespoons of softened vanilla ice cream into the centre of each soufflé. Decorate with the orange zest or sprigs of mint and serve.

Serves 4
Preparation time: *10 minutes*
Cooking time: 10–12 *minutes*
Oven temperature: *150°C/300°F/Gas
  Mark 2*

*kcal 116 • KJ 489 • protein 3 g
• fat 3 g • CHO 19 g*

clipboard: Slices of fresh orange or crystallized orange would both make an attractive decoration for this chocolate soufflé and would reinforce the orange liqueur.

Dairy produce

Quark

Edam

Low-fat cream cheese

Quark

Quark is a curd cheese which has a pleasantly creamy texture, in spite of the fact that it is particularly low in fat. It is made in Germany and Austria. White in colour with a smooth spreadable texture, it is similar to cottage cheese. It can be used in many sweet and savoury dishes.

Edam

Edam cheese is one of the best-known of the Dutch cheeses. It is made from cow's milk and has a slow fermentation period. It is a softish cheese, free from holes, and is covered in red wax. It is fairly low in fat and reduced-fat versions, which are still lower in fat, are also available.

Low-fat cream cheese

A soft white, smooth-textured cheese made from milk and cream, cream cheese is delicious with bread or incorporated into a dressing for potatoes and salads. The low-fat variety has had its fat content reduced and is therefore the best choice when you are following a low-fat diet.

Skimmed milk

Low-fat yogurt

Virtually fat-free fromage frais

Low-fat crème fraîche

Skimmed milk

In order to be labelled skimmed, milk must be skimmed of as much fat as possible, until the fat content is less than 0.5 per cent. Skimmed milk contains just as much calcium as full-fat milk and is therefore as nutritious.

Low-fat yogurt

Yogurt is of great benefit to the digestive system. It can be either natural or fruit-flavoured. It is also available in low-fat or non-fat versions and is used in numerous ways in many sweet and savoury dishes in cuisines all over the world.

Virtually fat-free fromage frais

Fromage frais is a low-fat soft white cheese from France. Its consistency depends very much on its fat content, and a virtually fat-free version is now available. It can be eaten by itself or used in cooking, or served as an accompaniment instead of cream.

Low-fat crème fraîche

Crème fraîche is cream to which a lactic acid bacteria culture has been added. This has the effect of thickening the cream, as well as giving it a characteristic sharp flavour. It can be used in many sweet and savoury dishes, and is a good substitute for soured cream. Low-fat crème fraîche has had some of the fat skimmed off and is therefore much lower in fat than full-fat crème fraîche.

Apricot Cheesecake

425 g/14 oz can apricot halves in natural juice
6 orange jelly cubes
250 g/8 oz carton Quark
75 ml/3 fl oz natural low-fat yogurt
apricot jam, warmed and sieved, to garnish
1 tablespoon flaked almonds (optional)

Biscuit base
125 g/4 oz digestive biscuits
50 g/2 oz low-fat spread

line the base of an 18 cm/7 inch sandwich tin with greaseproof paper. Strain the juice from the apricots into a jug. Make up to 150 ml/¼ pint with water, if necessary. Pour the liquid into a small saucepan and bring to the boil. Add the jelly cubes and stir until dissolved. Return the jelly to the jug and leave to cool.

choose 10 apricot halves for decoration and set aside. Purée the remaining apricots with the Quark and yogurt in a blender or push them through a sieve. Stir in the cooled jelly.

pour the mixture into the sandwich tin and place in the refrigerator for 2–3 hours to set lightly.

crush the digestive biscuits. Melt the low-fat spread in a pan and stir in the crumbs. Spread this over the cheese base evenly, pressing it down gently. Leave the cheesecake in the fridge for about 6–8 hours until set.

dip the tin into warm water for a few seconds to loosen it before turning out the cheesecake. Invert the tin on to a flat plate and turn out the cake. Decorate with the reserved apricot halves, glaze with warmed apricot jam, and top with almonds, if liked, though these will increase the fat content.

Serves 8
Preparation time: *30 minutes, plus setting*

***Kcal** 179 • **KJ** 754 • **protein** 7 g • **fat** 5 g • **CHO** 28 g*

Whole Strawberry Ice Cream

3 egg yolks
1 tablespoon redcurrant jelly
1 tablespoon red vermouth
300 ml/½ pint plain natural yogurt
375 g/12 oz ripe strawberries, hulled
4–6 strawberries with stalks, halved, to garnish

put the egg yolks into a food processor with the redcurrant jelly, vermouth, yogurt, and half the strawberries, and blend until smooth.

transfer the mixture to a shallow container, and freeze until the ice cream starts to harden around the edges.

tip the ice cream back into a bowl and beat to break up the ice crystals. Chop the remaining strawberries and mix into the semi-set ice cream. Return to the container and freeze until quite firm.

scoop the ice cream into stemmed bowls or glasses and decorate each one with strawberry halves.

Serves 4
Preparation time: *25 minutes, plus freezing*

Kcal 132 • KJ 553 • protein 7 g • fat 5 g • CHO 15 g

Fresh Lime Sorbet

This is a beautiful colour and has an unbelievably fresh and welcome flavour – just the thing for those hot summer days.

3 limes
175 g/6 oz caster sugar
600 ml/1 pint water
1 egg white, stiffly whisked

pare the rinds of the limes with a potato peeler, reserve and squeeze the juice. Dissolve the sugar in the water and bring to the boil. Boil for 3 minutes. Add the lime rinds and boil for a further 3 minutes, uncovered and fast. Remove the lime rinds and set aside.

cool then add the lime juice. Strain into a freezerproof polythene carton and freeze until mushy. Stir thoroughly, mixing the sides into the centre, then carefully fold in the stiffly whisked egg white. Refreeze, covered, until firm.

serve in bowls, decorated with the reserved lime rinds, with biscuits, such as tuiles d'amandes.

Serves 4
Preparation time: *20 minutes, plus freezing*
Cooking time: *6 minutes*

kcal 177 • KJ 757 • protein 1 g • fat 0 g • CHO 46 g

Breads

Flour, grains and pulses

Puy lentils

Bulgar wheat

Buckwheat flour

Granary flour

Bulgar wheat
Bulgar wheat is made from wholewheat grain, including the wheatgerm, and is therefore rich in protein, mineral salts and carbohydrates. It has a distinctive flavour and is frequently used in many vegetarian dishes, including salads and stews.

Buckwheat flour
Buckwheat flour is made from roasted buckwheat seeds and is often used in pancakes, blinis, crisp thin cakes and Asian soya noodles. Buckwheat seeds came orginally from central Asia but the buckwheat plant is, in fact, a native of the Soviet Union.

Granary flour
Granary and wholemeal flour containing bran are healthy options as they are rich in roughage and vitamins. Freshly milled granary flour has a nutty aroma and gives a strong texture to bread. It is often used in yeastless breads, such as Irish soda bread.

Puy lentils
Lentils are the small, round, dry, flat seeds of the lentil plant. They are particularly rich in carbohydrates, protein, phosphorus, iron and B vitamins, and are a good addition to a child's diet. They can be used in soups, casseroles, salads, or as an accompanying vegetable, the flavour of which goes especially well with pork. The green Puy lentil is grown in France and has a particularly good flavour. Lentils have the great advantage that they do not need soaking before being cooked, which makes them a particularly convenient choice.

Kidney beans

Red split peas

Pinto beans

Canned chick peas

Red split peas

These are small dried peas, which have been split in two. Like many pulses, they are especially rich in carbohydrates, proteins, phosphorus and potassium, and therefore play an important part in a healthy diet. They should always be soaked before cooking, and are often used in soups and stews. They are also available canned.

Pinto beans

The pinto bean is a variety of kidney bean. It is a pale colour with red markings. It is used in many Mexican and Spanish dishes. It is available dried or canned.

Kidney beans

These are the seeds of the haricot bean and are glossy, a characteristic dark reddish brown colour, and shaped like a kidney – hence the name. They are used in spicy dishes such as chilli con carne and in many other Mexican and Spanish dishes, and are also good cold in salads. They are available either dried, in which case they need soaking before being cooked, or canned, which are obviously much more convenient. Like most other pulses, they are highly nutritious and are particularly rich in carbohydrates, proteins, minerals and B vitamins.

Chick peas

Chick peas are the round, pea-like seeds of a leguminous plant. They are available dried, in which case they need soaking, and canned. They are rich in carbohydrate, protein, phosphorus, calcium and iron. They are used in soups, stews and salads.

Wholemeal Soda Bread

250 g/8 oz plain flour
1 teaspoon bicarbonate of soda
2 teaspoons cream of tartar
2 teaspoons salt
375 g/12 oz wholemeal flour
300 ml/½ pint milk
4 tablespoons water
flour, to sprinkle

sift the plain flour, bicarbonate of soda, cream of tartar and salt into a mixing bowl. Stir in the wholemeal flour, then add the milk and water and mix to a soft dough.

turn on to a floured surface, knead lightly, then shape into a large round about 5 cm/2 inches thick.

place on a floured baking tray, cut a deep cross in the top of the loaf and sprinkle with flour. Bake at 220°C/425°F/Gas Mark 7 for 25–30 minutes. Cool on a wire rack.

Makes 1 x 675 g/1 lb 6 oz loaf (12 slices per loaf)
Preparation time: *20 minutes*
Cooking time: *25–30 minutes*
Oven temperature: *220°C/425°F/Gas Mark 7*

per slice: *kcal 166 • KJ 705 • protein 7 g • fat 1 g • CHO 34 g*

clipboard: To cook in a microwave, place on a large greased plate. Microwave on Medium (50%) power for 5 minutes, giving the plate a half turn twice. Increase the power setting to Full (100%) and microwave for a further 3 minutes, giving the plate a half turn twice. Allow to stand for 10 minutes before transferring to a cooling rack.

Fig Loaf

This is a deliciously moist loaf, thanks to the addition of figs and treacle.

125 g/4 oz bran flakes
125 g/4 oz dark soft brown sugar
125 g/4 oz dried figs, chopped
2 teaspoons black treacle
300 ml/½ pint skimmed milk
125 g/4 oz self-raising flour

put the bran flakes, sugar, figs, black treacle and skimmed milk into a bowl. Mix well together and leave to stand for half an hour. Sift in the flour, mixing well.

put the mixture into a greased 500 g/1 lb loaf tin and bake in a preheated moderate oven at 180°C/350°F/Gas Mark 4 for 45–60 minutes.

turn out of the tin and allow to cool. Serve sliced, and spread with low-fat spread, if liked.

Makes 1 x 500 g/1 lb loaf (8 slices per loaf)
Preparation time: *20 minutes, plus standing*
Cooking time: *45–60 minutes*
Oven temperature: *180°C/350°F/Gas Mark 4*

per slice: *Kcal 170* • *KJ 725* • *protein 5 g* • *fat 1 g* • *CHO 39 g*

Date Loaf

250 g/8 oz dates, chopped
175 ml/6 fl oz cold tea
250 g/8 oz wholewheat flour
4 teaspoons baking powder
1 teaspoon ground mixed spice
175 g/6 oz soft brown sugar
1 egg, lightly beaten
1 tablespoon demerara sugar

put the dates in a bowl, pour over the tea and leave to soak for 2 hours. Add the remaining ingredients, except the demerara sugar, and mix thoroughly.

turn into a lined and greased 1 kg/2 lb loaf tin. Sprinkle with the demerara sugar and bake in a preheated oven at 180°C/350°F/Gas Mark 4 for 1–1¼ hours.

leave in the tin for 5 minutes, then turn on to a wire rack to cool.

serve sliced and spread with low-fat spread, if liked.

Makes 1 x 1 kg/2 lb loaf (15 slices per loaf)
Preparation time: *10 minutes, plus soaking*
Cooking time: *1–1¼ hours*
Oven temperature: *180°C/350°F/ Gas
   Mark 4*

per slice: *kcal 1228 • KJ 1227
   • protein 6 g • fat 2 g • CHO 67 g*

Granary Bread

1.5 kg/3 lb malted granary flour
2 teaspoons salt
2 sachets dried yeast
1 teaspoon brown sugar or black treacle
900 ml/1½ pints warm water
beaten egg, to glaze
a little buckwheat, for sprinkling (optional)

mix together the flour, salt and yeast in a large warmed bowl. Add the sugar or treacle to the measured water in a bowl, and stir into the flour to make a soft pliable dough.

knead the dough on a lightly floured surface for 10 minutes until smooth and elastic. Return to the clean bowl and cover with lightly oiled clingfilm, or a polythene bag. Leave in a warm place for 1 hour, or until the dough has doubled in bulk.

turn the dough on to a lightly floured surface and cut in half. Knead each piece until smooth, then place in two 1 kg/2 lb loaf tins. Place the tins in a large, lightly oiled polythene bag and tie loosely. Leave in a warm place to prove until the dough rises above the sides of the tin.

brush the loaves with beaten egg and sprinkle with buckwheat, if using. Bake in a preheated oven at 220°C/425°F/Gas Mark 7 for 30–45 minutes. Leave to cool on a wire rack.

Makes 2 x 1 kg/2 lb loaves (15 slices per loaf)
Preparation time: *30 minutes, plus proving*
Cooking time: *30–45 minutes*
Oven temperature: *220°C/425°F/Gas Mark 7*

per slice: *Kcal 163 • KJ 694 • protein 6.4 g • fat 1 g • CHO 34 g*

Stocks and Dressings

Chicken Stock

1 whole chicken carcass
3.6 litres/6 pints water
1 teaspoon salt
1 Spanish onion, peeled and stuck with 4 cloves
2 celery sticks, chopped
2 carrots, coarsely chopped
2 sprigs of parsley
1 bouquet garni
1 bay leaf
8 black peppercorns

put the carcass into a deep saucepan, cover with the water and add the salt. Bring to the boil, skimming off the scum with a slotted spoon. Lower the heat, partially cover the pan and simmer for 1 hour.

add the onion, celery, carrots, parsley, bouquet garni, bay leaf and peppercorns. Stir and continue simmering, partially covered, for a further 1½-2 hours. Add more water if the level drops below the bones.

cool slightly. Remove the carcass, then strain the stock through a fine sieve into a bowl, discarding all the vegetables and herbs. After straining the stock, pick over the carcass, remove any meat still on the bones and add it to the stock.

leave to cool, then skim off the fat with a spoon or blot with kitchen paper. Cover the stock, refrigerate it and use within 3 days. This stock is suitable for freezing – if frozen use within 3 months.

Makes about 3.6 litres/6 pints
Preparation time: *5–8 minutes*
Cooking time: *about 2½–3 hours*

(with fat removed) *kcal 98 • KJ 408
• protein 12 g • fat 5 g • CHO 2 g*

Vegetable Stock

3 medium potatoes, chopped
1 medium onion, finely sliced
2 leeks, chopped
2 celery sticks, chopped
2 medium carrots, chopped
1 small head of fennel, finely sliced
thyme, parsley stalks and 2 bay leaves
1.5 litres/2½ pints water
salt and pepper

put all the vegetables into a pan with the herbs and the water. Bring to the boil slowly, then skim. Add salt and pepper to taste. Simmer for about 1½ hours, covered,

skimming the stock three or four times during cooking.

strain the stock through clean muslin or a very fine sieve. Cool and store in the refrigerator until required.

Makes about 1 litre/1¾ pints
Preparation time: *10 minutes*
Cooking time: *1½ hours*

kcal 46 • KJ 190 • protein 2 g
• fat 3 g • CHO 2 g

Fish Stock

1 kg/2 lb fish trimmings
1 small onion, peeled and finely chopped
2 leeks, chopped
1 bay leaf
parsley stalks, sprigs of fennel and lemon rind
1.2 litres/2 pints water
200 ml/7 fl oz dry white wine
salt and pepper

place the fish trimmings in a large saucepan with the onion, leeks, bay leaf, parsley stalks, sprigs of fennel, lemon rind and water. Bring to the boil slowly, then skim any surface scum.

add the white wine, and salt and pepper to taste and simmer very gently for 30 minutes, skimming the stock once or twice during cooking. Strain the stock through clean muslin or a very fine sieve. Cool and keep chilled until needed.

Makes about 1 litre/1¾ pints
Preparation time: *15 minutes*
Cooking time: *45 minutes*

kcal 50 • KJ 200 • protein 0 g
• fat 0 g • CHO 0 g

Tomato Sauce

1 medium onion, chopped
2 tablespoons olive oil
1 garlic clove, crushed (optional)
750 g/1½ lb tomatoes, skinned and seeded
1 tablespoon chopped basil
150 ml/¼ pint red wine or Chicken Stock (see page 244)
½ teaspoon soft dark brown sugar
1 tablespoon tomato purée
½ teaspoon grated orange rind
salt and freshly ground black pepper

fry the onion gently in the oil for 3 minutes. Add the garlic, if liked, and the tomatoes and basil, and cook together for a further 2 minutes.

add the remaining ingredients and simmer gently for 25 minutes, until the sauce is soft and pulpy.

press the sauce through a sieve.

reheat the sauce if a hot sauce is required; otherwise cover it and store in a refrigerator.

Makes approximately 400 ml/14 fl oz
Preparation time: *10 minutes*
Cooking time: *30 minutes*

each of 6 portions: *Kcal 82 • KJ 345 • protein 1 g • fat 4 g • CHO 6 g*

clipboard: This sauce is much easier to sieve if it is first blended in a liquidizer or food processor.

Low-Calorie French Dressing

2 tablespoon olive oil
6 tablespoons wine vinegar
½ teaspoon mustard
¼ teaspoon sugar
salt and pepper

place all the ingredients, with salt and pepper to taste, in a screw-top jar and shake vigorously until well blended.

Makes 125 ml/4 fl oz
Preparation time: *5 minutes*

per dessertspoon: *Kcal 12 • KJ 49 • protein 0 g • fat 1 g • CHO 0 g*

Homemade Yogurt

600 ml/1 pint semi-skimmed milk
1½ tablespoons natural low-fat live yogurt

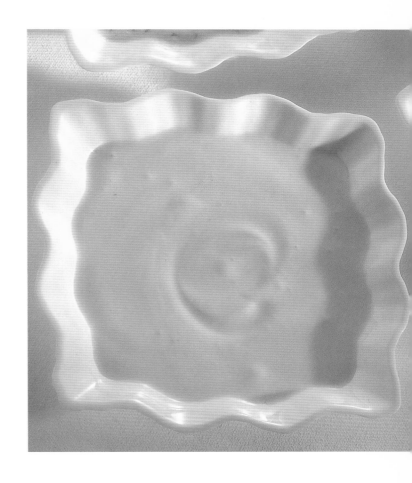

put the milk into a pan and bring just to the boil; allow to cool to blood heat.

lightly whisk in the live yogurt until thoroughly mixed.

pour into a wide-necked vacuum flask, and seal securely.

leave to stand undisturbed for about 10 hours or overnight.

keep the yogurt in the refrigerator for up to 4 days.

Makes about 600 ml/1 pint
Preparation time: *10 minutes, plus fermenting*
Cooking time: *1 minute*

each of 6 portions: *Kcal 53 • KJ 225 • protein 4 g • fat 2 g • CHO 6 g*

clipboard: Yogurt is a fermented milk product. The fermenting agent is a little fresh yogurt, which is added to the milk. You can, of course, use your own homemade yogurt as the fermenting agent for making more.

Tomato Juice Dressing

125 ml/4 fl oz tomato juice
125 ml/4 fl oz wine vinegar
1 teaspoon grated onion
½ teaspoon dried mustard
½ teaspoon sugar
½ teaspoon Worcestershire sauce
1 teaspoon chopped fresh parsley
salt and pepper

beat the tomato juice with the vinegar, grated onion, mustard, sugar, Worcestershire sauce, parsley and salt and pepper, to taste, until well blended. Alternatively, place all the ingredients in a screw-top jar and shake vigorously to combine well before using.

Makes 250 ml/8 fl oz
preparation time: *10 minutes*

kcal 54 • KJ 228 • protein 2 g • fat 1 g • CHO 10 g

Lemon and Yogurt Dressing

150 g/5 oz natural low-fat yogurt
1 tablespoon lemon juice
2 tablespoons chopped mixed fresh herbs
salt and black pepper

combine all the ingredients in a bowl, whisking well with a fork.

cover with cling film and chill in the refrigerator until ready to serve.

Makes 200 g/7 oz
Preparation time: *5 minutes, plus chilling*

kcal 90 • KJ 377 • protein 89 g • fat 1 g • CHO 12 g

clipboard: There are many possible variations on this dressing. Use mint instead of mixed herbs for cucumber salads, basil for tomato salads and parsley for green salads or potato salads.

Low-Calorie Vinaigrette

2 tablespoons lemon juice
3 tablespoons olive oil
1 teaspoon Dijon mustard
1 garlic clove, crushed
1 tablespoon chopped fresh parsley (optional)
1 tablespoon fresh chopped chives (optional)
salt and freshly ground black pepper

beat the lemon juice with the olive oil, mustard, garlic, chopped herbs, if using, and salt and pepper to taste, until well blended. Alternatively, place all the ingredients in a screw-top jar and shake vigorously to combine well before using.

Makes 75 ml/3 fl oz
Preparation time: *5 minutes*

per dessertspoon: *kcal 32 • KJ 130
• protein 3 g • fat 3 g • CHO 0 g*

Slimmer's Blender Mayonnaise

1 egg
salt and pepper
½ teaspoon dried mustard
4 tablespoons olive oil
2 tablespoons lemon juice

place the egg, salt and pepper and mustard in a blender. Process for a few seconds. Remove the centre cap from the lid and gradually add the oil with the motor still running on low speed.

gradually add the lemon juice until the mixture is thick. Serve at once or keep for up to 1 week in a screw-top jar in the refrigerator.

Makes 100 ml/3½ fl oz

per tablespoon: *kcal 49 • KJ 200 • protein 0 g • fat 5 g • CHO 0 g*

clipboard: Ring the changes according to what you are serving this with. For a curry mayonnaise, for example, replace the mustard power with curry powder to taste. For a herb mayonnaise, add ½ tablespoon of very finely chopped fresh herbs after the lemon juice.

Index

Acknowledgments

Photo Credits
Simon Smith: front jacket
Simon Smith: back jacket

Special photography by Simon Smith

All other photos:
Octopus Publishing Group Ltd. / William Lingwood, Jean Cazals, Chris Crofton, Philip Dowell, Laurie Evans, Sue Jorgensen, Graham Kirk, Sandra Lane, Fred Mancini, Hilary Moore, Vernon Morgan, Roger Philips, Roger Stowell, Clive Streeter, Philip Webb, Paul Williams

Special photography home economists
Lucy Knox and Sarah Lowman

Jacket home economists
Lucy Knox and Sarah Lowman